PRAISE FOR *REWR*

"*Rewriting Eve* is a treasure. Ronna Detrick is part archaeologist and part astronaut. She writes to excavate ancient stories and make them fresh, alive, and meaningful again. She journeys to the wild edges of imagination to dance with these women under an expansive star-lit sky. In reclaiming these voices of wisdom and hope she offers each of us the gift of showing the way back home to our own deepest knowing."
—CHRISTINE VALTERS PAINTNER, PhD, online Abbess of AbbeyoftheArts.com and author of twenty books including *Birthing the Holy: Wisdom from Mary to Nurture Creativity and Renewal*

"Hope is a courageous discipline these days, and to revision a limiting story is a bold and hopeful act. A story can create and destroy worlds. A once-upon-a-time can be a battering ram that breaks a long-held dam, one that kept the most medicinal, archetypal rivers from feeding and healing us. To that end, Ronna's book is an epic achievement and essential addition to any apocalypse-savvy library."
—DANIELLE DULSKY, Founder of The Hag School, author of *The Holy Wild, Seasons of Moon and Flame*, and *The Sacred Hags Oracle*

"As I read *Rewriting Eve*, I kept thinking of all the women who have grown up in churches that don't allow women to be pastors, preachers, or priests. Then I thought about all the women who have gotten as far away as possible from Christian churches because of Christianity's widespread anti-feminism. Rewriting Eve is a tremendous gift to both groups. It opens up the Bible in a fresh, liberating, stereotype-challenging way. Whoever you are, you will feel that Ronna Detrick is your pastor in these pages, and the best Bible teacher you ever had."
—BRIAN D. McLAREN, American pastor, speaker, and author of *Faith After Doubt and Do I Stay Christian?*

"I've been waiting for this book my whole life. Or rather, I've been waiting for this book from the first moment I could tell there were voices missing. No, not just in Sunday School. There, sure, but elsewhere too. Boardrooms, media, you get the idea. And while this book holds a gift in the retelling of voices reclaimed, it also invites a bigger question for me: what other voices are missing? That is the invocation. To bring those voices forward . . . and mine too. Brilliantly written, lovingly crafted, this book is a calling forth and a revelation."
—TANYA GEISLER, Leadership Coach and Speaker

"The stories we've been told and tell ourselves about who we are as women shape our future, opening and, too often, closing possibilities. Ronna has written a stunning reimagining of our sacred stories using groundbreaking research. I savored this beautiful book and hope it will free us to rewrite all the stories that have silenced and shamed us."
—JENNIFER LOUDEN, author of *Why Bother?* and *The Woman's Comfort Book*

"This book will help you rewrite your own story. If you've carried the weight of a patriarchal religion on your shoulders, this book will lighten the load and give you the freedom to dance. I wish I'd had it in my twenties, but I'm glad I have it now."
—HEATHER PLETT, author of *The Art of Holding Space: A Practice of Love, Liberation, and Leadership*

"Ronna's book is an inspirational guide to awaken and renew your engagement with the stories of women in the Bible that often have been, like the 10 Commandments, fixed in stone. Many of us learned to accept without question what we were taught and did not welcome our own imagination. Ronna, like Eve, bites into the apple and breaks the rules as she helps us imagine the gifts wrapped in the rich and often hidden stories of biblical women. She gives us full permission to see, weave and claim our own stories, realizing we have a lineage of women who have traveled before us and are cheering us on."
—GAIL WARNER, MA, MFT, author of *Weaving Myself Awake: Voicing the Sacred Through Poetry*

REWRITING
EVE

REWRITING EVE

Rescuing Women's Stories from the Bible
and Reclaiming Them as Our Own

RONNA J. DETRICK

SHE WRITES PRESS

Published 2023
Printed in the United States of America
Print ISBN: 978-1-64742-561-6
E-ISBN: 978-1-64742-562-3
Library of Congress Control Number: 2023907948

For information, address:
She Writes Press
1569 Solano Ave #546
Berkeley, CA 94707

Interior Design by Tabitha Lahr

She Writes Press is a division of SparkPoint Studio, LLC.

For Emma Joy and Abby. No matter how many stories I tell, yours are the most awe-inspiring, beautiful, and sacred of them all. I love you.

In the old stories, it is women who make the world;
why then shouldn't we remake it?
—SHARON BLACKIE

CONTENTS

INTRODUCTION

Whether we know it or not, whether we have read them or not, whether we believe them or don't, our daily lives take direction from stories that are hundreds, even thousands of years old.
—ELIZABETH LESSER, *Cassandra Speaks*

To rewrite anything is an act of hope. An email, a text, a letter, a birthday card, a term paper, a story, a book, a love note. It is a striving to say what we truly mean. It is an internal desire to "get it right." It is precision and sometimes poetry. It is writing and writing nearly the same thing over and over again. It is tedious and exhausting, rewarding and exhilarating. It is a commitment to a better, stronger, clearer, and more eloquent and beautiful way to express what we truly think and deeply feel. It is a choice, a practice, a discipline. It is, by its very nature, endless.

We are constantly rewriting ourselves as a practical expression of hope. We rewrite the past to make sense of our choices (and others') and to make different ones moving forward. We rewrite our inner dialogue to enable healing and growth. We rewrite our vocation, our calling, our destiny, our future. We rewrite our relationships—those failed and those that fulfill. We rewrite our stories through therapy, journaling, self-reflection, even dreaming. We rewrite our own stories to make our way in the world, to find our place, to feel at home with who we are.

This has always been the way of it: stories are rewritten and retold, time and again. Around an outdoor fire or a kitchen table. Whether we sit in circle or on a pew. Whenever we spend time with family or friends. "We understand that story is not the gospel truth, or journalism, or courtroom testimony. . . . The fish gets a little bigger, the storm gets a little wilder, the love gets a little stronger, our bravery or disappointments get a little exaggerated in the telling over time."[1] And yet, for all this, we have made sacred stories and texts somehow off-limits to rewriting. They are carved in stone, inviolate, and immutable. To touch them, let alone tamper with them, will ruin them and us (or so we've been told). Our imagination is dangerous. These texts are sacrosanct, their retelling sacrilegious.

I believe exactly the opposite: When we do not dare to rewrite our sacred stories and texts, *we lose hope*. Our imagination is what keeps them alive and vital. But when we hold them at arm's length, when we declare that their meaning, value, and worth can only be maintained through objective distance, they become increasingly irrelevant—as do the institutions by which they are protected and ostensibly "revered."

I am not willing to lose hope. I rewrite sacred stories so that the women within them are seen again and anew—their voices heard, their harm named, their shame lifted, their silence ended, their perseverance esteemed, and *their hope* honored. And when that happens, everything changes. *We* change. We are seen, our own voices are heard, our own harm is named, our own shame is lifted, our own silence ends, our own perseverance is esteemed, and our own hope is not only honored but also fanned into flame—despite every attempt to tamp it (and us) down.

It is *my* deepest hope that as I rewrite these sacred stories of women, you will better see and understand your own. It is my deepest hope that you will bravely name the stories you've been told and the ones you tell yourself, and that you will rewrite them both—defiantly and on your own terms. It is my deepest hope that you will hold fast to every invitation to reimagine, reclaim, revision, and redeem the stories that form your sacred lineage, the shoulders upon which you stand, the women from whom you descend. And it is my deepest hope that you will know with unquestionable certainty that you are their daughter, their lineage, their kin.

Why these stories, particularly?

The stories that have meant the most to me, that I remember and return to, are those in which I catch a glimpse of myself between the lines. Sometimes it is a character and the way their life reflects a particular aspect of my own: a challenge, a loss, a miracle, a fantasy. Other times it is brilliant prose that exquisitely captures my emotions, questions, needs, or hopes. And then there are the times when I get lost in the plot and am transported into a place that is intimate and real. In the best of them, I turn the last page or watch "The End" scroll across the screen and feel seen and heard, acknowledged and known. Neil Gaiman captures this perfectly in *M Is for Magic*: "Stories you read when you're the right age never quite leave you. You may forget who wrote them or what the story was called. Sometimes you'll forget precisely what happened, but if a story touches you, it will stay with you, haunting the places in your mind that you rarely ever visit."[2]

But there is another whole world of stories that has impacted me (and you, as well) even more profoundly. Family legend, tradition, and lore craft our beliefs and serves as the foundation to our memory. Historical narratives inform our understanding of culture, gender, race, sexuality, politics, and the world at large. Myths swirl in and out of our conscious awareness. Childhood fairy tales shape our hopes and dreams. And all of these, whether we are conscious of them or not, determine the ways in which we make sense of our lives: our relationships, our behaviors, our proclivities, our likes and dislikes, our opinions, our expectations . . . *everything*.

Of them all—read, heard, told, inherited, and imbued—the stories of women in scripture are those that have impacted us the most. This is a bold claim to make, and one that I wish I could deny. Even the words "women in scripture" cause a visceral and impossible-to-ignore reaction that feels important to name. Your response may be a sense of gratitude, a comfortable acknowledgment of a Text you've known, revered, and loved. Or perhaps, instead, you feel your claws come out and your defenses go up at their mere mention. (If it helps, my reaction is a bit of both.) No matter what, our response where these women and their stories are concerned is neither indifferent nor benign. *It is exactly this that validates their impact, power, and significance*—for good and, yes, for ill.

The sacred stories of women have rarely been told in ways that honor the perspective and experience of the women themselves. They have been misunderstood, neglected, and frequently maligned. They have been coopted and trapped within systems of male power and privilege. These same systems have shaped a history of oppression, silencing, and exclusion—sometimes even the contents of the bible itself (written *by* men *for* men).

When we pull back even the slightest bit, we must acknowledge that none of this is unique to biblical interpretation alone; rather, it reflects the general condition of women worldwide, for centuries and still today. Which is, of course, my point.

The way these women's stories have been told (or not) correlates directly with the realities women face—past, present, and future. They are woven into our collective consciousness, our individual subconscious, and our cultural history; they are the water in which we swim. Elizabeth Lesser, quoted in the epigraph at the top of this introduction, says, "You may think these stories are the stuff of 'once upon a time' and have nothing to do with you or your times. But 'once upon a time' is now, because the past is laced into the present on the needle and thread of stories."[3]

We can choose how to respond to this truth. We could decide that these stories (and the larger text within which they reside) are too damaged, too indoctrinated, and completely irrelevant; we could turn and walk away. But there is a vast difference between rejecting the doctrine and dogma—even the ideology of those who have been telling the stories—and walking away from the women themselves. When we throw out the proverbial and patriarchal bathwater, we perpetuate centuries-old harm. It is the exact opposite of what they deserve, what *we* deserve. "The patriarchy, so afraid of female power—and shouldn't that give us hope?—that they went to extravagant length to suppress it, created new stories to cover it up."[4]

Another response is to listen to the women themselves. Instead of turning away, we can turn toward them, draw closer, and breathe them in. We can imagine how *they* want their stories told, how they want their circumstances and choices understood, what they want us to know, still and always. We can invite and allow their emotions, their voice, and their heart on our behalf. We can come to believe that they reside in our midst, are present, and *stay*. We can trust that they offer us what we have longed for, sometimes even without knowing: evidence of the feminine—its sacredness and power. A sacredness that is accessible, tender, and strong; a power that has been present from the beginning of time, will not be silenced or quelled, and is ours to claim. This response is the harder path, to be sure; it is an uphill battle and climb. There is much to wade through, much to dispel, much to decry, and much to grieve. But these ancient, sacred women and their stories are worth every effort.

In 1972, American poet, essayist, and feminist Adrienne Rich spoke to the necessity of this effort through the lens of literary critique:

Re-vision—the act of looking back, of seeing with fresh eyes, of entering an old text from a new, critical direction—is for women more than a chapter in cultural history: it is an act of survival. Until we can understand the assumptions in which we are drenched we cannot know ourselves. And this drive to self-knowledge, for women, is more than a search for identity; it is part of her refusal of the self-destructiveness of male-dominated society. . . . We need to know the writing of the past and know it differently than we have ever known it: not to pass on a tradition but to break its hold over us.[5]

Not just Adrienne Rich, but many more besides. Feminist, liberation, and womanist theologians have been interpreting (and rewriting) scriptural texts in profound and transformative ways for decades. With impressive skill and expertise, they parse out the smallest grammatical truths hidden in verb tense, gendered nouns, the placement of subject and object, and so much more. They uncover deep—and, often, *avoided*—meaning. They look at the broad, sweeping context of theology itself (the study of the nature of God and religious belief)—how it has been nearly exclusively shaped by and on behalf of white men; how that has dramatically and painfully altered the text and our interpretation of it. They tirelessly work to "break [tradition's] hold over us." Wilda C. Gaffney, a brilliant theologian and expert in "womanist midrash," perfectly captures the spirit of this effort:

I am talking back to the text, challenging it, questioning it, interrogating it, unafraid of the power and authority of the text, just as a girl-growing-into-a-woman talks back to her elders, questioning the world around her in order to learn how to understand and navigate it.[6]

Resistance to this idea often shows up in the belief that scriptural texts are objective, that this collection of history and myth, letters and poems, is unbiased and untouched other than by the very hand of God. I am not one to discount the possibility of the miraculous, but my unswerving creed is that all storytelling is subjective—even *and especially* the stories in scripture. When committed to the tenets of inerrancy or absolute truth, we tend to forget that these stories were passed down from generation to generation for thousands of years, held in memory alone, before a single one was written down. And even then, words were subjectively dictated to a scribe who made his own subjective decisions along the way. Within Hebrew and Greek, the original languages of the Old and New Testaments, the slightest pen stroke, the inadvertent misplacement of a jot or tittle, or a misspelled word had the potential to significantly alter intended (and subjective) meaning.

Every bit of this is gift and grace. Subjectivity allows us to find meaning in a sacred text that we may have discounted long ago as too misogynistic, too painful, too peripheral. Subjectivity gives us *carte blanche* permission to reimagine and rewrite these stories in ways that reflect a woman's internal and external realities, that honor the women themselves—and us as well. And subjectivity enables us to hear these women speak today... because they can, because they must, because that is what the best stories always do.

Despite a long history of oppression, silencing, and shame, these women and their stories inexplicably persist. They are brave, wise, vulnerable, and gentle—just like us. They have known tremendous loss, fear, and pain—just like us. They have been overlooked and underestimated—just like us. They have been misunderstood and dismissed—just like us. They have survived—just like us. And not only a few, but countless numbers—women named and unnamed, known and barely heard of, shocking, heartbreaking, defiant, broken, bold, triumphant, incredible.

From these endless numbers, I have chosen just ten:

XX ✿ REWRITING EVE

Eve
Cain's Wife
Hagar
The Midwives
Jael
Vashti
Esther
The Canaanite Woman
The Woman at the Well
The Woman of Revelation 12

Each of them has a story to tell, wisdom to impart, and hope to lavish. Each of them gifts us with profound and relevant perspective on our own story, our choices, and the life we deserve to live. Each of them, *all of them*, come alongside to imbue courage and strength. They offer comfort and consolation when we feel unheard, unseen, and alone. They remind us to persevere and rise above all that keeps us tamed, small, and disempowered. They shout a deafening "no" when we are harmed. They sing a glorious "yes" when we embrace the legacy that is ours. They stand—regal, immutable, and sovereign—in a world that desperately needs their voices, their presence, their beauty, and their power; in a world that desperately needs ours, too.

As I said at the start, the stories that I remember and return to are those in which I catch a glimpse of myself between the lines—in which I feel more seen and heard, acknowledged and known. These *are* those stories, and this is my "why." I can hardly wait for you to know them as I do, to experience just how deeply *they* know *you*. I long for you to feel them reach out and take your hand—even more, inhabit your heart. And I trust that they (and this book) will offer you far more than just a glimpse of yourself between the lines; rather, you will recognize them as an impossible-to-ignore mirror of who you truly are—their daughter, their lineage, their kin.

AND YET, TENSIONS ABOUND.

For all that I love about these women's stories, they present particular difficulties. First is the biblical text in and of itself. I have no need to disparage a book that many view as sacred and sacrosanct. Author and practical theologian Rachel Held-Evans captures my thoughts exactly: "I have come to regard with some suspicion those who claim that the Bible never troubles them. I can only assume this means they haven't actually read it."[7] At the same time, I do not want anyone to run screaming into the dark at the very mention of the words "biblical text" before turning the pages that follow. If I could, I would extrapolate these stories from the pages in which (and by which) they have been bound. Still, this *is* where they reside. We need a starting point from which to build *and* to deconstruct. I encourage you to read each story as though it were the first time (which perhaps it is)—to do all you can to suspend both disbelief and frustration just long enough to journey with me somewhere new and far more expansive. I promise, that *is* where we are headed.

A second tension is talk of God. It is possible that I carry enough ambivalence about this for all of us combined, but please know that *I know* it is a dicey topic. As such, no part of me will be remotely disturbed by your resistance, your tension, your beliefs, or your disbelief. Simultaneously, I hope you are both challenged and compelled, for that is the result of all good writing and every good story. And these *are* good stories. I encourage you to take ample liberty in substituting any language for the divine that resonates. And if none will suffice (or even when it does), may the women themselves be an expression of the sacred on your behalf. For this is exactly what they are, what they offer, and what they invite.

A third tension is inherent in looking closely at stories that reveal blatant and painful disregard for women. But to not tell them for that reason feels even more injurious: we risk them slipping further into the depths of oblivion, and eventually being completely erased from our memory—and if that happens, all the harm that has been perpetuated on them (and us) over the centuries will have been for naught. I encourage you to take deep breaths, allow in as much as you can, extend yourself grace, and hold fast to the demand that no such stories should have ever been lived through in the first place or ever again.

A fourth tension is revealed in the fact that I am a white, able-bodied, straight, cisgender woman who has known and benefited from incredible privilege in each of these categories. Even with an ongoing commitment to name and acknowledge the harm that my entitlement has caused (and does still), I am certain there are limitations to the ways in which I've attempted to apply these stories to women of today—contexts I have missed, nuances I have overlooked, cultural traditions and perspectives I have not taken into consideration, gender and sexuality applications that are not as inclusive as I hope or intend. The work I am doing to free these texts from patriarchy and misogyny is, of course, the tip of the iceberg. I have not gone far enough. You deserve to see yourself within them. Forgive me for the places in which I have fallen short in this regard; I deeply desire to learn and change.

There are undoubtedly more, but for now, the final tension I am aware of is what I feel within. I am trying to balance intelligent and thoughtful critique with fiery and passionate opinions. I am trying to balance my longing to impart wisdom and inspiration with my known tendency to argue in order to make a point. And I am trying to balance my deep desire to honor the women in these ancient, sacred stories with my endless prayer that it is *your story* you come to see, claim, and honor most clearly and powerfully of all. So, one last time, I encourage you to look past my efforts and my failings, past the places where I struggle and even where I might succeed. For in the end, what matters most is that you encounter these women for yourself—that you hear their voices speaking directly to you in mind and heart, that you feel their embrace, that you sense their presence as close as your

own breath, that you walk through your world with the unshakeable awareness that you have never, *ever* been alone, and, above
all else, that you actually believe them when they say, "You are
our daughter, our lineage, our kin."

How to read this book:

The ten stories that follow are ordered as they are in the bible
itself. Though you need not read them sequentially for them to
make sense and offer meaning, there is value in considering how
the stories and lives of women did (or did not) change over time.
Within each chapter you will find the following:

- An opening reflection that sets the stage for this
  woman's story.
- The biblical text—paraphrased for understanding,
  vocabulary, and ease of reading.
- A series of vignettes that speak to the realities of this
  woman's life and our own, predominant interpretations and cultural impact, and the wisdom and hope
  she offers still.
- A personalized blessing—my imagining of her voice
  on your behalf.
- Reflection questions that invite you deeper into your
  own story through the lens of hers.

Whether you read this book through in one sitting, use it as
companion and support over a longer period of time, or pick it up
again and again for perspective and encouragement, fold down
the corner of pages, write in the margins, underline, highlight,
ask even more questions than I have, and assume, if not believe,
that every single woman within is holding her breath in antici-
pation of who you are yet to become knowing she is endlessly
by your side.

MY HOPE AS WE SET OUT.

In her book *Out of Sorts: Making Peace with an Evolving Faith*, Sara Bessey says, "And here, at last, as we sit among the questions still unanswered and the path you must walk ahead, I pray for your journey as it unfolds into the unknown. I know you feel a bit out of sorts. We all do sometimes. It's okay. Don't be afraid. You are so very loved. I pray you would remember it, know it, live it, breathe it, rest in it: beloved."[8]

I love this prayer. It speaks perfectly to mine on your behalf. May the pages that follow *not* answer your every question but rather gift you with more curiosity than ever before. May you fan your desire into flame, no matter what, believing it to be DNA-level proof of the legacy from which you descend. May you encounter a sense of the sacred that defies everything you have ever been told and surpasses everything you've ever hoped. May you discover that there is more than one way to tell and rewrite a story—*especially* when it comes to your own. May you be companioned by wise and amazing women, in the flesh and in realms unseen, that remind you of who you truly are, *especially* on the days you forget. And may you confidently walk through your world knowing, without a shadow of doubt, that you are loved. Remember this, know this, live this, breathe this, rest in this. Always.

May it be so.

—RONNA DETRICK
Hampstead, NC
October 2023

Chapter One: EVE

A woman will not leave her garden until she harbors a deep knowing, planted there at the base of her spine, that she deserves better.
—DANIELLE DULSKY

There are very few stories we know by heart, stories we instantly and intuitively recognize as undeniably true. Not true as in factual or provable; true as in resonant, wise, and worth trusting. On the rare occasions when we hear them, we step into a secret garden, a waking dream. We breathe deeply. We feel more like ourselves than ever before. We gasp in near disbelief at all that we finally see, understand, and know with clarity, even certainty. These stories inexplicably capture and articulate our every ache *and* our every hope. They awaken us to what is authentic and real, to what we have, somewhere within, longed for all along. These are stories our heart knows.

One of them belongs to Eve.

Not the story that instantly comes to mind. Not the one that has shame written between every line. Not the one that has been twisted into oppressive doctrine and dogma. Not the one that is wielded to make us believe we are not enough or too much. Not the one we'd rather *not* hear, thank you very much. Instead, a story reimagined, retold, and heard by heart. The one that invites us into our own story and life. The one in which Eve meets us, takes our hand, and welcomes us home.

HER TEXT
—paraphrased from Genesis, chapters 1–3

Long before time began, only darkness existed. In one magnificent moment or infinite forever, Spirit began to create. Dark was separated from light and water from sky. Sun and moon formed a rhythm of day and night. Trees, plants, and animals were imagined and enlivened. A human, ʾāḏām, Adam, was shaped from the dust of the earth, life breathed into him by Spirit. Then one culminating divine and creative act took place: while the man slept, one of his ribs became the starting point for ʾiššâ, woman. When he awoke and saw her, he could only respond with wonder and awe.

Creator saw all that had been made and said, "It is very good."

One day, a serpent asked the woman if they were allowed to eat the fruit of any tree. "No," she said. "We are not to eat from the tree in the center of the garden or we shall surely die." The serpent told her that this was not true; on the contrary, upon eating the fruit her eyes would be opened and she would be wise. Not one to turn down wisdom, she took the fruit and ate it, then gave some to Adam, who was with her; he ate it as well. Their eyes were, indeed, opened and they saw that they were naked, arummim, which means unconcealed, innocent, and with no guile.

Creator walked through the garden in the cool of the day and called out, "Where are you?" When there was no answer, Creator asked if they'd eaten from the tree. The man said, "Yes, but it was her fault—the woman

that you gave me." Then the woman told how the serpent had deceived her. Hearing this, Creator cursed the
serpent and named consequences for the humans—an
articulation of what their life would hold from this point
forward. For the woman, pain in childbirth, desire for her
husband, and submission to his will. For the man, endless
and futile toil in his work.

A flaming sword was placed over Eden's entrance, keeping
them safe from the Tree of Life; the world beyond the
garden's borders became their home. Never abandoned
or alone, the Creator clothed them, protected them,
stayed with them, and loved them. As they left all they
had known and entered into all that was yet ahead, Adam
named the woman *ḥaûâ*, Eve, *the mother of all life*.

I WISH I COULD SIT BESIDE YOU as you read Eve's story—that we could talk, late into the night, about where your mind wanders, every emotion that is summoned, every tangent that deserves to be followed, every story of your own that is somehow remembered and piqued. In the absence of such, I can imagine . . .

You are reminded of why you never liked this story much, why you never gave it much credence, and/or why you shake your head in disbelief when you encounter those who do. So much races through your head and heart: the serpent's seeming trickery, their hiding, Adam blaming Eve, Eve blaming the serpent, the consequences, being banished, the flaming sword. You are trying to recall what I left out, what I changed, where I took liberties. You are definitely stuck on "your desire will be for your husband, and he will preside over you." You feel, deeply, all the pain women have known throughout time because of this story, the pain you have known. And if this was your first time reading this tale in its entirety, you are incredibly grateful that it has *not* been part of your learned heritage or faith tradition!

I know. And I understand. Despite the *many* times I've heard Eve's story told and read it for myself, my thoughts and feelings have not lessened or dulled. I react. I rage. I reflect. These days, more than all else, I reimagine—but it's taken me a long time to get here.

When I was young, I never questioned the Genesis story or thought of it as anything other than true, even literal. I was never curious about why Adam and Eve were forbidden to eat from one particular tree, why God created it in the first place, and why it was then disallowed. I never asked why the serpent was often described as "subtle, shrewd, crafty, and sly" when God had declared everything "good." I never wondered why Adam was told they would die if they ate the fruit, when *clearly* that didn't happen. I never thought to examine any of this, because what I *did* know with certainty was that it was wrong to question the bible. That would be tantamount to what Eve did. And look where that led!

I knew that Eve was wrong to listen to the serpent, to take the fruit, to eat it, and most of all to tempt Adam with it. I knew that she was disobedient; after all, they were banished from Eden because of her singular choice. I knew that because of her, my responsibility was to *not* follow her example, to somehow undo her mistake by not making any myself. I knew that my intuition, my desire, my wisdom, and even my heart could not and should not be trusted. And I knew that if I was to hope for any better outcome than the one she'd forced upon all of us at the beginning of time, I needed saving—by a man, by the male god, and *from* myself.

Whether or not your childhood was like mine; whether your faith tradition was the same, different, or completely nonexistent; whether you've heard Eve's story a thousand times or just this once—it has shaped your life as much as it has mine. It has "served" as the predominant religious ideology, normative cultural template, and overarching social framework for nearly every aspect of the Western world. It is not a stretch to claim its impact and presence within the realities women face, like unequal pay, fewer leadership positions, domestic violence, sexual harassment and trafficking, unraveling abortion rights, and more. All of these are informed and influenced by an inherent understanding of women that, though often unspoken, is no less living and active for the silence around it.

Yet none of this is *because* of Eve herself, or even her story!

"History isn't what happened," says noted women's historian Sally Roesh Wagner. "It's who tells the story."[1] And the *storytellers*, particularly as it relates to Eve's story, have nearly all, if not exclusively, been men.

Let's take a brief walk through history:

Tertullian, the father of Latin Christianity, 2nd century:
> And do you not know that you are (each) an Eve? ... You
> are the devil's gateway; you are the unsealer of that (for-
> bidden) tree; you are the first deserter of the divine law;
> you are she who persuaded him whom the devil was not
> valiant enough to attack. You destroyed so easily God's
> image, man. On account of your desert—that is, death—
> even the Son of God had to die.

Augustine, the Bishop of Hippo, Doctor of the Church and Latin
Father, 4th century:
> [W]oman was given to man, woman who was of small
> intelligence and who perhaps still lives more in accor-
> dance with the promptings of the inferior flesh than by
> superior reason. Watch out that she does not twist and
> turn you for the worse. What difference does it make
> whether it is in a wife or in a mother, provided we none-
> theless avoid Eve in any woman.

Thomas Aquinas, Doctor of the Church, 13th century:
> As regards the individual nature, woman is defective and
> misbegotten, for the active force in the male seed tends
> to the production of a perfect likeness in the masculine
> sex, while the production of woman comes from a defect
> in the active force or from some material indisposition,
> or even from some external influence.

John Calvin, French theologian, pastor, and Protestant Reformer,
16th century:
> [The] woman was created afterwards, in order that she
> might be a kind of appendage to the man; she was joined
> to the man on the express condition, that she should be

at hand to render obedience to him. . . . God did not create two chiefs of equal power, but added to the man an inferior aid. . . .

John Knox, Scottish theologian, minister, and Protestant Reformer, 16th century:

Woman in her greatest perfection was made to serve and obey man. . . . Nature, I say, paints [women] further to be weak, frail, impatient, feeble, and foolish, and experience has declared them to be inconstant, variable, cruel, and lacking the spirit of counsel and regiment.

Napoleon Bonaparte, French military and political leader, 19th century:

Nature intended women to be our slaves. They are our property.

Episcopalian Bishop C. L. Meyers, when faced with the question of the ordination of women in the Church, 20th century:

The sexuality of Christ is no accident nor is his masculinity incidental. This is the divine choice.

Norman Mailer, American novelist, journalist, playwright, and filmmaker, 20th century:

A little bit of rape is good for a man's soul.

Pat Robertson, American media mogul and televangelist, 20th century:

Feminism encourages women to leave their husbands, kill their children, practice witchcraft, destroy capitalism, and become lesbians.

James Dobson, conservative Evangelical leader, 20th century:

[This is the] greatest threat to the family in my lifetime. It will represent the most radical, atheistic, and anti-family crusade in the history of the world. [It will] undermine the family, promote abortion, teach immoral behavior to teenagers, incite anger and competition between men and women, advocate lesbian and homosexual behavior, and vilify those with sincere religious faith. . . . This is Satan's trump card if I have ever seen it. (In response to the 1985 United Nations Conference on Women.)

Donald Trump, former President of the United States, 21st century:
It is a very scary time for young men in America, where you can be guilty of something you may not be guilty of. . . . Women are doing great. You've got to deny, deny, deny, and push back on these women. If you admit to anything and any culpability, then you're dead. . . . You've got to be strong. You've got to be aggressive. You've got to push back hard. (On the #MeToo Movement.)

And if this weren't enough, on women in general, Donald Trump said:
Women have one of the great acts of all time. The smart ones act very feminine and needy, but inside they are real killers. The person who came up with the expression "the weaker sex" was either very naive or had to be kidding. I have seen women manipulate men with just a twitch of their eye—or perhaps another body part.

Deep breath. . . .
I sometimes worry that I am overzealous in my unswerving belief that the *telling* of Eve's story *has and does* determine the treatment of women past and present—that perhaps I am taking things too far. But then I reread these quotes—along with many more besides—and am reminded that nearly every example of

women's silencing, shame, and status (or lack thereof) is rooted here, in one singular story. It is tempting to walk away, even from Eve herself—to throw out the whole damn thing. But what I have come to see and experience is that every bit of the endless pain and misunderstanding that has resulted from her story's telling invites me to healing and deeper understanding, an undoing of the past and a rewriting of the future. When I accept this, the blatant disregard and disdain for Eve (and too many women throughout time) becomes my most profound source of hope, a determined pursuit of all women's honoring. And the acknowledgment that Eve's story, as it is most often told, has caused centuries of upset and disruption allows me to dream of what is possible when it is reimagined and retold for good. She has proven her capacity to change *everything*! Which means she can yet again, which means that you can as well.

"The women who have been locked inside the books they called *good* deserve liberation from their externally imposed immorality," writes Danielle Dulsky. "We must unlock the cages in which they have been contained for so long, trapped behind the iron bars of judgement and dismissal. We women of this evolving world are tasked with their redemption, for they are we."[2]

May it be so.

I often imagine how Eve must long for her story to be told—everything she wishes we had understood and honored over time. I imagine the woman she longs for us to see, understand, and trust. I imagine all that she wants us to know and believe— yes, about her, but much more so about ourselves. I imagine she stretches out her arms, draws us in, and holds us tight.

More than I imagine, I *know*.

Eve reverberates off of dusty pages, traverses centuries of silence and shame, and enters into our very souls. She inhabits our consciousness, our bloodstream, our very being. She offers us the most generous wisdom and beautiful truth. She extends us an endless invitation to what was always intended for us since the dawn of time. She compels us to recognize her as the closest of companions who will infinitely empower, strengthen, inspire, and heal.

When Eve's story is told *her* way—when we take it in, trust it, and make it our own—everything changes. We have the courage to move past every perceived restraint into something big and vast and delicious. We trust our gut, our intuition, our deep, inner truth. Even more, we act: we step forward, reach out, and take a bite of the very thing that defines our future. We are compelled by a passion that does *not* end in disaster and infinite curse but rather in wide-open possibility. And we are confident that we do none of this alone.

Have I mentioned that Eve changed everything? She still does. And as her daughter, her lineage, her kin, we can do the same.

YEARS HAVE PASSED, BUT I CAN STILL picture my daughter's tear-stained face and hear her ragged, scratchy voice as she pronounced the worst possible fate: she was not popular *enough*, not pretty *enough*, she would never be *enough*! I had obliquely expected this conversation to take place by the time she was a teenager, but as memory serves, it happened in first grade.

Hearing my child speak those words, I felt enough rage to burn the house to the ground—better yet, the school itself. When my youngest came home a couple years later with her own version of the same, I struggled to withhold my wrath from the perpetrators, the playground, the entire planet. In both instances, and so many more that were yet to come, I held my daughters close and wiped away their tears. I reminded them of who they *truly* were—and that to characterize them as anything less was a lie from the pit of hell. I told them of their inherent beauty, value, and worth, and that those things could not, would not, be defined by someone else's opinion, smallness, or pain. Still, no matter what I said, I could not erase what they had heard, what they had internalized, what they believed.

I wish I'd had the wherewithal to tell them of Eve. I wish I'd recounted what was *always* true about her, no matter what anyone else ever thought or said throughout time. I wish I'd helped them hear *her* voice on their behalf, again and again. My daughters are now in their mid-twenties—amazing and strong, confident and awe-inspiring, reflective of the divine, to be sure. And yet, if asked, they would confirm the lingering echoes that cause them to hark back to those earliest memories, the experiences that began to cement their sense of self as *not enough*. I, now in my early sixties, still fall prey to the same. My response may no longer be tears, insecurity, or blatant comparison to my peers, but it remains just as ingrained. I question my value and worth; the insipid presence of "not enough" continues to haunt.

Eve's story, told as is, leaves us striving. We believe that we will somehow be rescued from the tyranny of "not enough" if we just try a bit harder, become a bit better, and continuously attempt to please others. Surely if we are good enough, pretty enough, perfect enough, enough-period, Eden—or at least a place that feels less fraught with unmet expectations and endless disappointment (in ourselves)—will be within our grasp.

We would be well-served and profoundly healed to undo every bit of this—to start all over again.

IN THE BEGINNING . . .

There are two creation stories in the book of Genesis. In the first, man and woman are formed out of the earth itself—created together and simultaneously. In the second, the Creator says, "It is not good for the man to be alone. I will make a helper, ʿēzer, suitable for him." (Genesis 2:18) Though Eve is brought into being by the divine in both, in the latter version, she is almost an afterthought: taken from man, formed of and for man, inferior to man. When this telling takes precedence, it is not difficult to understand why women have been viewed and treated in less-than-equal, less-than-honoring ways. Nor is it surprising that we are tempted to view and treat ourselves the same.

Eve invites us to look again.

In the first account, we witness the nature of creativity itself. Spirit begins broadly, separating light from dark and sky from water. With each morning and evening cycle, things become more sophisticated, more developed, more complex. The man is formed out of the dust of the earth, breathed into by the divine's very self. And at last, saved for last, the creation of woman.

When we cast our eyes beyond just this story, we see this pattern everywhere. A painter's first work is nothing like what they bring into being after years of practice. What Beethoven composed as a child cannot compare to the masterpieces he crafted near the end of his life. Through perseverance, discipline, and time, a writer's skill evolves and strengthens; she gets better and better. Even in science and technology, ideas and inventions that were once impossible to conceive of are now second nature and commonplace; we continue to advance in vast and exponential ways. All creativity has an upward arc. It gains momentum and increases in sophistication, complexity, and beauty.

When we return to and reimagine Eve's story through this lens, she is penultimate—the highest and best reflection of the divine. She is *not* the one who marred the divine's intention or plan, upset the apple cart, and caused the downfall of all humanity. She is the fullest and most complete expression of creation and the Creator's very self. And if her, so too, my daughters, me and you.

You reflect the divine. Imagine if the dominant beliefs about women throughout history were nothing close to what was quoted above—"weak, frail, impatient, feeble, and foolish . . . inconstant, variable, cruel, and lacking the spirit of counsel and regiment." *You reflect the divine.* Imagine how different your life would be if these four words had been spoken over you by parents, grandparents, siblings, lovers, bosses, friends, culture—if they had never been argued, doubted, or denied. *You reflect the divine.* Imagine how different our world would be if this was what we witnessed and affirmed in all of humanity. *You reflect the divine.*

"It takes courage to kiss a snake and a soulful audacity to sink one's teeth into the forbidden fruit," writes Dulsky, "but to look back and honor those moments as moving benedictions to the wild within you is a . . . particular and glorious victory."[3] When you *do* imagine this, when you *believe* that, just like Eve, *you reflect the divine*, everything changes.

As it should. As it must. At last.

When reimagined and retold, Eve's story helps us see how unnecessary every bit of our self-doubt, even our self-loathing, is and has always been. When we acknowledge her as the Creator's final and best act, we give no credence whatsoever to childhood or present-day critique. We no longer search for Eden-like perfection but instead walk through our everyday world aware that the divine dwells infinite and immutable within us—manifested in and through our very presence. We silence every hiss of "not enough" when we listen to her voice, her wisdom, and her heart speaking on our behalf again and again: *You reflect the divine. You reflect the divine. You reflect the divine.*

And just like before, just as in her story, *everything* changes. As it should. As it must. At last.

———— ⟨⟨⟩⟩ ————

WHEN I WAS FIRST MARRIED, I CONSTANTLY and silently chose my husband's desire over my own. He didn't ask me to do this and certainly never demanded it, but I believed it was the right thing to do. And early on, it was easy! I was in love; my deepest desire was to do anything and everything possible to sustain our bliss. I defaulted to his preferences over my own. I didn't make waves when my opinions or feelings conflicted with his. My choices were consistently based on what I believed would make and keep him happy, *not* my desires for the same. I was convinced that if I gave heed to my desire—particularly when it was different or dissonant from his—he would not be able to handle it or me. My worst fears would be confirmed: I would be too much. No—I had to keep myself in check, bite my tongue, swallow my pride, and be a good and responsible wife. *Don't be Eve,* I thought. *Be amenable, generous, selfless, less demanding, less selfish; be undesiring of anything other than this.*

This is not to say that my desire had been subsumed or extinguished. It nudged me at times, poked its head out, raised the hair on the back of my neck. But I knew better: it was far too dangerous to name, let alone pursue.

To be clear, my desire was nothing close to what you'd read about in a romance novel—clandestine, wildly passionate, bodice-ripping, and out of control. What I desired was to be heard and seen, to be deeply understood, to be known and honored for who I was *becoming*, not the "me" I'd worked so hard to sustain, the woman I knew my husband depended on, the commitment I'd chosen over myself no matter the costs or compromises.

It took a very long time before I was able to see that my fear of being too much had turned our marriage into something that wasn't enough.

It was a normal Saturday morning. I was washing the dishes that remained after the girls' obligatory chocolate chip pancakes while compiling a mental list of chores to complete before day's end: clean the bathrooms, do the laundry, grocery shop, fix dinner, do more dishes. Up to my elbows in soapy water, I heard my husband ask me what I'd like to do for our fifteenth wedding anniversary— just weeks away. I could tell you of everything that led up to that moment: years of conversations, arguments, compromises, promises, misunderstandings, effort, disappointments, heartache, ambivalence, restraint, reason, return. I could tell you of so many moments just like this one: I'd debate, vacillate, argue with myself, and try to decide what to do and what to say, what *not* to do and what *not* to say. All I can tell you is that in that moment, everything fell silent but for a quiet, confident voice within that said, "Tell the truth, Ronna. Say what you *actually* want; what *you* desire."

I turned to my husband and said, "I'm done." And in that moment, my desire took precedence over my fear.

I'd love to tell you that what followed was glorious and redemptive. Instead, it was hugely disruptive, excruciating, and full of cost and consequence—as every divorce is, no matter the circumstances or intended congeniality. In the days, weeks, and months that followed, it was all I could do to cling to that single moment of clarity and courage, to keep listening to that voice— Eve's voice—within me.

IT IS A RARE WOMAN, INDEED, WHO has been affirmed for her desire or *ever* had it encouraged. Chances are slim to none that we have heard anyone say, *Want more. Ask for more. Demand more! Trust your desire and trust yourself!* More often than not, we have been told just the opposite: *Don't want too much. Don't ask for more. Don't demand anything. Don't get too full of yourself.* We've learned that trusting, pursuing, or *indulging* our desire only leads to disaster. Don't desire food; you'll gain weight. *Too much.* Don't desire attention, especially by using/raising your voice; it's unladylike and unwanted. *Too much.* Don't desire more money or dare to ask for a raise; you'll be seen as greedy and selfish. *Too much.* Don't desire or expect too much from love; you'll be disappointed and, at the very least, perceived as too needy. *Too much.* Don't desire sex (or dress like you do); you'll get what's coming to you and then be forever marked as *un*desirable. *Too much.* Don't desire equity, parity, equality, a seat at the table, or even respect; you'll be tagged as bitchy and domineering. *Too much.*

Regardless of background or beliefs, this is woven into our very DNA. To *not* desire, *not* want, has been deemed the saner, wiser choice for women. If we are to ever question such a thing, we only have to look at Eve's story to see the ramifications of our desire untamed. She has served as an ever-looming cautionary tale against the perils of desire. Or so we've been told. . . .

But it is exactly the opposite of this that Eve longs for us to know, understand, and trust. She longs for us to (finally) hear and believe her when she says, again and again: *Your desire is good. Your desire is good. Your desire is good.*

Our desire is *not* something to sublimate and ignore; it is all that is trustworthy and wise within us—an endless source of discernment and joy. Our desire, when fanned into flame, is reflective of who we truly are: created in the image of the divine *and* Eve's daughter, her lineage, her kin.

Much of the time, it is just too hard to believe. The inherent goodness—try as we might to listen to it, follow it, and trust it—collapses under the weight of feared outcomes. We resolve, yet again, that we are too much, and our desire is *bad*—a temptation we'd best avoid at any cost. If we ever dare to wonder or wander, we are quickly reminded, with incontrovertible evidence, that our desire is dangerous, problematic, and must be restrained. It's an easy leap—from eating the apple to banishment from Eden, from telling the truth to the certain demise of a marriage, from pursuing our desire to wreaking havoc on others' lives.

Easy, yes. Correct, no.

Eve's desire, when looked at closely, with compassion, and through her lens, has no such moral to her story. She graciously and generously offers us a template that makes sense of what we intuitively know and consistently experience. *Of course* our desire can be costly—*and* it is our strongest form of discernment and wisdom. *Of course* our desire is dangerous—*and* in the very best and life changing of ways! *Of course* our culture (patriarchy specifically) does everything in its power, including how it has told Eve's story, to keep us from unleashing it, honoring it, and acknowledging it—*and* you need not believe a word of it! *Your desire is good.*

"If women trusted and claimed their desires, the world as we know it would crumble," writes Glennon Doyle. "Perhaps that is precisely what needs to happen. . . . Maybe Eve was never meant to be our warning. Maybe she was meant to be our model. Own your wanting. Eat the apple. Let it burn."[4]

ONE OF THE MOST POWERFUL WAYS in which we initiate
change and transformation—in our own lives and in the world—is
to unequivocally name all that has kept us small, silenced, shamed,
or trapped, and then do exactly the opposite. It's a necessary discipline to contradict all that has been so deeply ingrained within
us, to defy any and everything that holds us down and back, to
literally upset the apple cart.

We do this at a systemic level by applying intelligent critique
to any policies, protocols, theologies, or politics that hinder
women's growth, self-expression, and inherent worth. We lobby.
We protest. We vote. And we persist. Sojourner Truth articulated
this perfectly when speaking at the Equal Rights Convention in
New York in 1897:

> If the first woman God ever made was strong enough
> to turn the world upside down all alone, these women
> together ought to be able to turn it back and get it right
> side up again! And now [that] they are asking to do it,
> the men better let them. Truth burns up error.[5]

The day after Donald Trump's inauguration in 2017, I attended
the Women's March. It was the largest single-day protest in US
history; worldwide participation was estimated at over seven
million. What a powerful experience to be surrounded by throngs
of women, men, and children—all of whom had come together
on behalf of women's rights, human rights, really. As I was jostled
and carried by the crowd, I remembered Eve. I wondered how
she felt about the whole thing—the pink hats, the sea of signs,
the electrifying speeches, the solidarity that swelled as so many
of us demanded that things be "turned right side up again." I am
certain she remembered the Garden, her unswerving clarity as

she honored her agency and desire, and the taste of the fruit. . . . And I am certain she smiled during those hours as so many of us gathered, grateful that we were tasting the same.

For as much as I loved being part of that day, I know the change we desire and deserve is far easier painted onto a sign than brought into being. And as much as I would like to (and do) blame Donald Trump and so many others like him for every limit, constraint, and lack of human rights that women have known throughout time, I also know that much of what holds us back comes from within.

My inner critic is alive and well. It has the uncanny ability to completely derail me, my confidence, my choices, and certainly my actions. It doesn't matter that I know it to be nothing more (and certainly nothing less) than an accumulation of patriarchal messages, doctrine and dogma that no longer serve, culturally reinforced misogyny, old stories, capitalism's endless effort to convince me that I am not enough, and my own laundry list of perceived failures, mistakes, and faults. Still, it natters on and shuts me down.

Until I remember Eve.

When I do, I can extend myself grace and acknowledge that this caustic voice within has, in large part, been shifted and shaped by poor tellings of her story—threads and themes that echo, *You're to blame. Don't trust yourself. You'll only wreak havoc if you follow your instinct. Stay inside the lines.* When I hear their hiss, something in me rises up, defiant and determined, hand-painted signs at the ready. It's as though she speaks through me, as though she's been waiting for the opportunity to set right all that has been turned upside down within me and my world. And sometimes I catch a whiff of something fresh and crisp in the air—an apple, maybe. . . .

Reimagining and remembering Eve's story is both a collective and personal act. It is a radical act. And it summons the change we so deeply desire—for all women, all humans, and most certainly ourselves. Indeed, "to get [the world] right side up again!"

SOMETIMES, OFTENTIMES, WE STRUGGLE to believe in our divinely decreed value and worth, not so much because of Eve but because of her god. Well, not *her* god, exactly, but the one of whom we've been told.

East of Eden—*after* Eve's choice—God's direct interactions, intimacy, and care increase exponentially. Beginning in Genesis 4, an epic story commences: scene after scene of God in conversation, in *actual* appearances, offering protection, presence, and love for generations. Eve's story, when retold, enabled the overarching story of scripture to be told in all three Abrahamic traditions—Judaism, Christianity, and Islam: a chosen people, cared for by the divine, delivered by their god into a promised land. And all of this after *and because of* Eve.

Eve's god does not demand our obedience or perfection but instead fully embraces our deepest intuition and bravest choices. Eve's god shows up, walks alongside us, and reminds us that our wisdom can be trusted—that *we* are trusted. Eve's god is not obsessed with sin but with reconciliation and relationship. Rather than require that we prove ourselves or be better or hold ourselves back or reign ourselves in, Eve's god reminds us, again and again, as does Eve, that *we reflect the divine* and *our desire is good*.

We should be thanking her instead of blaming her.

It's not too late.

EVE'S STORY—REWRITTEN, REIMAGINED, and redeemed—is what we need, desire, and deserve. It is the story of a woman created in the image of the divine, whose desire is good, and whose choices do not birth disaster. It is the story that frees us from every attempt at perfection, all striving for forgiveness, and every limiting self-belief. It is the story of our forebear, our mother, our mentor, our hope. It is the story that is and has always been waiting to welcome us home.

❤◇◇

Dear One:

My story, my true story, is one not of shame but of the beauty of desire. It is one not of abandonment or banishment but of embrace and belonging. It is one not of original sin, the Fall, or the danger of a woman's desire but of agency and courage and passion. And your true story, just like mine, isn't one of shame or banishment or sin. Not only yours, but your mother, her mother before her, any and every woman, forever and ever, amen.

Let my story, my true story, be the one you tell and live. Let my story, at last, invite you into all the beauty and strength that was always intended and always yours . . . juice from the ripest fruit dripping down your chin.

I see you as you are: beautiful and worthy, brave and wise, at home in your own skin, able to speak your mind and follow your desire and trust your heart. You are glorious— as you should be, as you deserve to be, as you've always been. You are my daughter, my lineage, my kin.

◇◇

QUESTIONS FOR
FURTHER REFLECTION:

1. Had you not yet read this chapter but simply heard me mention the name "Eve," what would your spontaneous response have been? Why? What has influenced and shaped how you feel about her story?

2. In what ways do your "beliefs" about her story mirror your beliefs about yourself?

3. How do you respond to the history of thought (Tertullian to Trump) related to Eve's story—the deeply ingrained beliefs about her and, subsequently, all women?

4. If you were to believe that, like Eve, you reflect the divine, how might that shape your sense of self, your inner thoughts, even your day-to-day choices?

5. What if your desire *is* good? If this is even remotely possible, what does it invite or inspire? What *do* you desire?

6. What risks or consequences might ensue if you upset the apple cart? In what ways are they keeping you from what you intuitively know to be right and true and wise? How might Eve's reimagined story impact or influence your choices?

7. Which do you feel most often: *not enough* or *too much*? How have these messages been ingrained and reinforced in your story through stories like Eve's (as it's been told)? What healing and change would ensue if you truly believed her insistence that you "are more than enough and cannot possibly be too much"?

8. How can you change, even transform, the way you are telling and living your own story, as inspired by Eve's rewritten and reimagined one?

Chapter Two: CAIN'S WIFE

[T]here are stories we will never find, no matter how many
times we search the sacred texts... And so we read between
the lines, listening beneath the layers of suppression and
neglect to hear the chorus of voices where we were told there
was only silence.

—JAN RICHARDSON

Almost a complete opposite to Eve—in terms of attention paid, stories told, and meaning applied—is Cain's Wife. It's almost as though she didn't exist at all.

Almost.

After Adam and Eve left the Garden, they had two sons, Cain and Abel. One day, in a fit of jealous rage, Cain killed his younger brother. His punishment was to wander the earth with no home and no family, a nomad. In fear for his very survival, he pleaded with the divine to protect him from those who would seek his death. God gave him a distinguishing mark that would forever keep him safe, and he settled in the land of Nod.[1]

That is nearly the end of what we know of him, except for one single sentence; fifteen words that change everything. . . .

Her Text

—paraphrased from Genesis, chapter 4, verse 17

Cain made love to his wife, and she became pregnant and gave birth to Enoch.

———————— ❧ ————————

It is an easy sentence to miss. If we don't stop, look closer, read between the lines, and reimagine the profound story that is hers, we miss even more:

> Cain's Wife is the first woman mentioned outside the Garden.
> Cain's Wife is Eve's daughter-in-law.
> Cain's Wife is married to a marked man.
> Cain's Wife gives birth to Eve and Adam's grandson.
> Cain's Wife is a mother who heard her husband's stories and told them to her son.
> Cain's Wife enabled countless generations to follow.

There is so much we miss in *our own* stories. It is easy for us to skip right over whole sentences, paragraphs, and incredibly powerful truths. We fall prey to naming ourselves in limited and limiting form: mother, wife, partner, employee. We diminish ourselves and/or feel overshadowed and overlooked.

Cain's Wife refuses every bit of this tendency and temptation. She reminds us that we descend from a long and brilliant line of women, herself included, who endure, who stay, who matter, who make a difference. She calls you, me, all of us, back to the truth that hovers between the lines, between the generations, between the stories told and those that are painfully mangled and misunderstood. She stands—solitary and distinguished—within one small sentence, and in doing so calls us to even more: out of the shadows, off of the page, and into the story and life that is ours. And if some day you decide to compile a list of sentences that even begin to capture the magnitude and magnificence of who you are, be sure to add this one:

You are Cain's Wife's daughter, her lineage, her kin.

THE FACT THAT *ANY* WOMEN'S STORIES made it into this text—are remembered at all—is miraculous. Especially one like that of Cain's Wife. When I consider the centuries over which the larger Judeo-Christian narrative has been told (and until relatively recent history, only orally) it is not hard to imagine how easily one small sentence could have been skipped. The storyteller, and later the scribes who copied down those same stories over and over again, could have completely overlooked it, jumped directly to her son, never included her in the narrative at all.

Even so, it *is* surprising that more has not been made of her— Eve's daughter-in-law. She and Cain would not have chosen each other, given that marriages in that place and time were arranged. Hardly a great catch or eligible bachelor women would have been lining up to meet, Cain was a loner with a distinguishing mark to keep him from being harmed (which assumes that people wanted to). Not only had he wandered far from his family to the land of Nod, he had no worth or inheritance to claim. How and why this woman's parents saw him as a suitable mate tells us at least something of how *she* was viewed and potentially even (de)valued. She would have known of her in-laws' beginnings, would undoubtedly have heard Cain retell his own bedtime stories about how his parents met, the fruit, the snake, and the journey into land they now knew as home. She would have sensed the dynamics between Adam and Eve—perhaps made tense by memory of what once was, certainly impacting her now-husband. She would have lived in the shadow of her husband's violent acts, his shame, his fear, and his life of forced isolation.

In between the little we know and all that we imagine is the vast and profound story of the woman who lived, loved, and survived within it. She deserves to be remembered.

I'm not always a fan of remembering. Quite frankly, there are plenty of things I would rather forget—plenty of East-of-Eden stories that have made me feel unseen, unheard, and insignificant. It is hard to acknowledge those chapters, to ask myself *why* I felt the way I did, to parse through what was circumstantial—cultural, familial, even religious—and what was and is mine to own and learn from. It is hard to revisit the pages in which I felt the ache of *not* being front and center, of *not* feeling noticed and valued as I wished and wanted—and how I responded (or didn't). It is hard to peer between the lines at the countless times I doubted my capacity, my choices, my very heart. In remembering Cain's Wife, I must remember myself—all of myself, even and especially the parts I'd rather ignore, repress, or gloss over.

It's not all that surprising that remembering slips through the cracks—especially when what we recall is hard to hold, hard to reconcile, and hard to heal—of our own stories and those of the ancient, sacred women who have preceded us: Eve, her daughter-in-law, and so many more. But when we choose to remember and reimagine, we are the ones who are restored. We remember ourselves—who we are, from whom we descend—and the legacy that is ours to sustain.

The mere existence of Cain's Wife, even in a single sentence, reinforces the incontrovertible truth that on some psychic, mythic, magical, and deeply archetypal level, her presence could not, would not, be forgotten. It reassures us that no woman's presence can be ignored—not for long, not ultimately, not really. We don't need there to be more to her story to know that this singular mention gives credence, value, and worth to *our* story, our life, and that of all women throughout all of time. It's as though she shouts, sings, and infinitely proclaims, "Look! I am here! I have survived this text! I have endured its tellers, its doctrine, its dogma, its frequent dismissal of (if not disdain for) women. I have lived, loved, and brought forth life. And never forget that I am here, still and always, with and for you."

So, on days or even in seasons when you feel invisible, inconsequential, *almost* forgotten, remember that this could not be further from the truth. One single sentence and one solitary woman proves otherwise. Cain's Wife calls you back to yourself, your significance, your very real and impossible-to-ignore presence, your place in this large and sweeping story—a story of which you are an integral and necessary part.

THERE ARE SINGLE SENTENCES THAT remain with us from the moment we hear or read them:

Happy families are all alike; every unhappy family is unhappy in its own way.
—LEO TOLSTOY, *Anna Karenina*

Ships at a distance have every man's wish on board.
—ZORA NEALE HURSTON, *Their Eyes Were Watching God*

When Mary Lennox was sent to Misselthwaite Manor to live with her uncle, everybody said she was the most disagreeable-looking child ever seen.
—FRANCES HODGSON BURNETT, *The Secret Garden*

It was the best of times, it was the worst of times . . .
—CHARLES DICKENS, *A Tale of Two Cities*

It is a truth universally acknowledged that a single man in possession of a good fortune must be in want of a wife.
—JANE AUSTEN, *Pride and Prejudice*

My appreciation for succinct and articulate prose has increased exponentially over the years. The more I read and the more I write, the more in awe I am of the beauty and power that can be captured with just a few words strung together.

That appreciation only increases when it comes to Cain's Wife. One sentence is all we have. And though we've barely given it a second thought, whole worlds dwell within it: *Cain made love to his wife, and she became pregnant and gave birth to Enoch.*

If we were in a creative writing workshop and I offered this sentence as a prompt, where would it take you? Would you speak of their relationship—Cain and his wife? Would you explore their lovemaking—its texture, its tenor, its passion (or its absence thereof)? Would you mention the quick leap from sex to pregnancy to birth, or would you slow the narrative down and wander into the blanks? Would you explore the meaning of Enoch's name ("dedicated") and what that tells us of his parents? Would you be curious about the fact that his mother is *not* named? Would you give her a name? What would it be? Would you wonder about why she was married to Cain in the first place—this murderous and marked man who was destined to wander the earth? Would you imagine what happened after her son was born and after that? Or would you write of yourself—the parents who brought you into the world? Stories of love . . . or not? Your experiences of labor and birth? Your desire for such? What it feels like to be unnamed?

All this from one single sentence.

When I was a teenager, my dad was determined to teach me skills he was certain I would need when out on my own, including how to change the oil in the car. I remember him bent over the open hood, showing me where the oil stick was and then expressing his frustration that I'd not grabbed a clean cloth before we started. He lay on his back under the car and pointed to the oil pan, loosened the bolts, and placed them, one at a time, into my open palm— except for the one I dropped. I can still hear it bouncing down through the engine, ricocheting off of parts whose names I'd never know, before eventually making its way to the garage floor and rolling out of his reach. He spoke one single sentence—not just that day, but other times, as well: "Think, Ronna Jo!"

This single sentence was code for whole worlds of meaning. I wasn't paying attention, wasn't taking things seriously enough, wasn't trying hard enough, wasn't living up to my potential, was disappointing him. Yes, related to the (never-to-be-used) skill of an oil change, but so much more besides: sustaining smart conversation at the dinner table, having intelligent opinions at the ready, using sarcasm as sharply as he did, performing with perfection at piano recitals and drill team competitions, attaining straight As. And it was wielded when it came to my writing—his critique of single sentences I crafted, structured, and slaved over.

It might seem odd that my father read my writing. Until, that is, you understand that he was a high school English teacher—*my* high school English teacher. I sat at a desk while he stood at the front of the room and taught the art of writing five-paragraph essays. Though he was determined to grade me fairly and equitably alongside my peers, the bar for me was definitely higher than it was for anyone else. Outside of his classes I had papers to write for other teachers—his peers and friends. I had college essays to compose and scholarship letters to send—a future to make happen. Everything hinged on the words and sentences I wrote. So when he said, "Think, Ronna Jo!" I knew I hadn't done enough. Above and beyond the issue at hand, the assignment that was due, or the lesson he was teaching (in class and otherwise), it sometimes felt that his love hung in the balance.

I still hear his voice when I write. I imagine exactly what he'd say about where I place a semicolon, whether or not a comma belongs before the "and" in a run-on sentence, how I have or have not held a consistent theme throughout a piece, a paragraph, a page. "Think, Ronna Jo!" I go back. I edit. I pull up the thesaurus in another tab on my computer to make sure I've chosen the *best* words to make my point. (Or should I say *finest* words, *optimal* words, *superlative* words, *foremost* words, *peerless* words, *unequaled* words?) I google if "high school" is one word or two. (It's two.) I pull up the Chicago Manual of Style to adhere to the rules of usage and grammar.

Though he's been gone for just over three years, were I able to ask him, he would tell me that my writing has far surpassed his every expectation and dream. He would tell me that he's totally forgotten about the dropped bolt and that a drive-through oil change is perfectly acceptable. He would tell me that I have done more thinking, and more deeply, than he could have ever imagined. He would tell me that I never disappointed him. He would tell me that he's sorry. And he would tell me that he wished he had more words, better sentences, whole tomes through which to express his pride, his joy, and his love. For as grateful as I am to know that every bit of this is true, that single sentence still holds sway.

My story is hardly unique. Consider the sentences others have spoken to you—and about you. What your father said that night at the dinner table. What your mother uttered as she turned her back and closed your bedroom door behind her. What your best friend whispered to someone else. The three words a lover did *not* speak. The passing comment you wish you could forget you ever heard but that now has your imagination working over-time, filling in the blanks, crafting story and meaning and entire scenarios without your consent, playing over and over again in your mind. Then there are the sentences that comprise your self-talk—one after another, in rapid-fire succession—the endless monologue that is often colored by contempt, guilt, insecurity, anxiety, and shame. Never mind that you would never say them to anyone you cared about; they race through your mind and lodge in your heart.

Such is the power of words—your own and others'. Spoken, screamed, sobbed, written, whispered, typed, texted, even inferred. Whole worlds held within them, especially when combined into sentences, scenes, stories, secrets held or told. But for all their power, they cannot capture the totality and expansiveness of who you are. Whether wound or blessing, they only depict the smallest part of just how vast and amazing you and your story truly are.

It is this that Cain's Wife invites and affirms: you are *so much more* than what others' words (or sentences) can possibly contain.

———— ⌘ ————

WHEN WE INTENTIONALLY REIMAGINE the ancient, sacred story of Cain's Wife, she receives that which she has always deserved: to be honored and esteemed. When we include her in our long and illustrious legacy of matriarchs, *our story* is the one that is strengthened and supported. When we see her, *we* are seen—no matter how small and insignificant we sometimes feel. Her "mere" fifteen-words hardly limit her expanse, her influence, her vastness, her import, her value, or her worth. And if her, so too us: her daughters, her lineage, her kin.

May it be so.

Dear One:

Nothing can erase your impact from this world. No silence nor untold story can hide you from sight. No darkness can cover your light. You are more than any single sentence could possibly hold or begin to describe.

Still, when moments and seasons of being unseen and unheard get the better of you, look for me. I am by your side, ushering your words to the page, your voice into the world, your presence into expression—unmistakable, unmissable, unforgettable.

And in all of this, always, only one sentence matters: you are my daughter, my lineage, my kin.

QUESTIONS FOR
FURTHER REFLECTION:

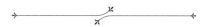

1. Her story is easy to forget. But so are ours—especially the stories we wish didn't exist or had gone differently. How does remembering Cain's Wife invite the significance of remembering (and maybe even rewriting) your own story?

2. What do you feel when you consider how easy Cain's Wife is to miss? What feels familiar about it? How does imagining and honoring her almost-missed story encourage you? What story might you write about yourself with the same amount of imagination and honor?

3. *You are not invisible.* This is far easier said than believed. What would be different in your day-to-day life if you held fast to this as undeniable truth?

4. Words have so much power. What are the sentences that have most impacted you, lodged in your mind and heart, continued reverberating over the years? And how might Cain's Wife's words—"*You are so much more than what others' words can possibly contain*"—offer you healing and grace?

5. If Cain's Wife's story, as small as it is, has so much relevance and impact, what truth does that reveal about your own? What would be different if you could see yourself as "large" as she is . . . and as she longs for you to know and believe?

Chapter Three: HAGAR

Wilderness can be at once a place of refuge and a space of disquietude. It can be where you both sigh in relief and feel your heart pounding nearly out of your chest as you approach the unknown.
—*Rachel Held Evans*

Few of us live lives that transition from "once upon a time" to "happily ever after." But when that is the story we are told and promised, it's not surprising that we are often disappointed, even a little bit lost. We wonder why *our* life does not come close. And we wander—as if in a desert. We long for respite from yet another mirage, search for signs of life, and pursue any direction that even attempts to make sense of the story we are *actually* living, the one that feels very far from what we expected or hoped. Maybe if we had been told stories of women who did *not* get kissed by a prince (or a frog), who did *not* get rescued. Maybe if we had been told stories of women who felt as lost as we do, who knew the desert intimately, who struggled to make sense of their own lives. Maybe if we had been told stories of women who saved themselves—gritty and raw and relatable, nothing perfect or princess-like about it.

Hagar's story is about as far from a fairy tale as we can get. Just as with Eve's, I grew up hearing it told in a particular way with specific lessons to be learned. But when I found myself in a desert of my own, those texts—as they'd been told and taught—no longer consoled, their "truths" no longer applied, and any sense of the divine felt close to nonexistent.

It was here, in the most desolate of places, that I encountered Hagar anew. Better said, it was here that she found and rescued me. I have never been the same. And the desert has never been more beautiful.

Her Text
—paraphrased from Genesis, chapters 12, 15–17, and 21

Life continued outside of Eden. Generations were birthed—descendants of Eve, *the mother of all living.* A man named Abram entered into this epic, sweeping drama, called by his god to leave his country, his people, and everything he'd ever known for another land. This calling was accompanied by a promise: "I will make you into a great nation, and I will bless you; I will make your name great, and you will be a blessing. I will bless those who bless you and all peoples on earth will be blessed through you."

So, at age seventy-five, Abram set out on his journey—along with his wife, Sarai, his brother, Lot, and all their possessions and servants. Many miles were traversed. Much time passed. Despite the promise, they were childless.

Abram said, "Sovereign Lord, you have given me no children, so a servant in my household will become my heir." In response, God said, "Your heir will be your own flesh and blood. Look up at the sky and count the stars, if indeed you can. So shall your offspring be."

More miles. More time. Still no child.

Out of desperation, Sarai took matters into her own hands and told Abram to sleep with Hagar, her Egyptian slave. When Hagar conceived, Sarai was not grateful, as expected. Instead, she said to Abram, "I put my maid in bed with you and the minute she knows she's pregnant, she treats me like I'm nothing." In answer, Abram said, "Your maid is your business."

Sarai took her anger out on Hagar, brutalized her even
with physical violence.[1] But Hagar chose to liberate herself
and ran away. Alone and afraid, she stopped near a spring.
And there, a messenger of God—"God in disguise, or
perhaps better, God in (human) drag"[2]—found her and
said, "Go back to your mistress and submit to her. I will
give you descendants too numerous to count. You will give
birth to a son. Name him Ishmael, for the Lord has heard
of your misery. He will be a wild ass of a man, and his hand
will be against everyone and everyone's hand will be against
him. He will live in hostility toward all his brothers."

Hagar named the god who spoke to her *El Roi* and said, "I
have seen the One who sees me." Then, with the knowledge
that her child would be protected and blessed, she returned
to Abram and Sarai and soon gave birth to Ishmael.

More miles. More time. And finally, at ninety years of age,
Sarah (her name changed in intervening years) gave birth
to a son of her own. She named him Isaac, which means
"laughter," for she said, "Everyone who hears of this will
laugh with me. Who would have believed that I would
yet nurse a child?"

The two boys grew up side by side. Sarah watched them
together and said to Abraham (whose name had also been
changed), "Get rid of that slave woman and her son, for
he will never share in Isaac's inheritance." Abraham was
distressed but did what Sarah demanded: he sent Hagar
and Ishmael away with nothing but some food and a skin
of water.

Now Hagar wandered the desert yet again, this time with
her son by her side. When their water ran out, he began to

cry. She placed him under a bush, sat down some distance away, and wept, unable to watch him die.

God heard the boy crying and appeared to Hagar for a second time, saying, "What is the matter, Hagar? Do not be afraid. Lift the boy up and take him by the hand, for I will make him into a great nation."

God was with the boy as he grew up. Years later, Hagar found him a wife from Egypt.

In the Qur'an, Ishmael is honored as a prophet and ancestor to Muhammad, the father of Islam. As promised, he is a "great nation," indeed. Hagar is remembered as an Egyptian princess, given or sold to Abram at one point in his journey. She has been revered as "the symbol of downtrodden women who persevere."[3]

———— ⟨❦⟩ ————

MY SPIRITUAL DIRECTOR—A WISE, QUIET, and deeply reflective Jesuit nun—asked me a question one day that changed my life: "What do you think Hagar would say to you in *your* desert, Ronna?"

I'd been wandering in it for quite some time by then, in session after session in which I argued, fussed, and fought over how to make sense of my marriage, whether or not to leave, how to stay. Simultaneously, I was in a faith crisis. There was too much I could no longer believe. I was raw with doubt and anger. I felt abandoned by what had promised to strengthen and sustain. In sum, my life was arid and parched—no visible sign of a god or angels, let alone water or hope. I prayed. I begged. I pleaded. I desperately longed to be seen and heard, rescued and blessed. Yet no voice spoke, no divine messenger or "God in [human] drag" appeared—I received no answers.

Still, I could not escape her question—and ultimately, it served me more profoundly than I could have ever asked or imagined. Eventually, I stopped arguing about unmet promises by a male god and embraced the gift and grace inherent in the story of a woman, in the story of Hagar, in the desert itself.

That same day, I sat down at my computer and started writing. I'd filled pages and pages by the time I stopped—line after line and paragraph after paragraph in which I heard Hagar's voice on my behalf, words that moved from my head to my heart and then onto the screen. It was magical and mysterious, spiritual and sacred. The more permission I gave myself to reimagine Hagar's story from *her* perspective, the more it related to *my* story. The more I felt her companionship and compassion, the more I felt my own wisdom and courage.

In time, I began to ask questions of her as though (and because) she was right beside me. In the midst of my day, when I wanted to run away, I asked her how she knew when to leave.

When I felt the hot sand burning my feet, I asked her to tell me about *her* desert—all that she thought about and felt, how she survived. When all I could do was sit and weep, I asked her what to do, what to pray, what to hope. When I could not see which way to turn, I asked her to be my compass, to give me some sense of direction and discernment for next steps. Unlike the seemingly silent god I'd been wrestling with for years, she was viscerally present and vocal, a fierce advocate and friend. She is, still.

It was another five years before I left that desert and entered another, before I left my marriage and became a single mother of two, before I exchanged the religion I'd known for a wide-open wilderness. But by then I had learned, even in the most cursory of ways, to follow both Eve and Hagar's lead, to trust *my* desire and *my* knowing, to believe in *my* wisdom and *my* strength. By then I had learned that I was met, comforted, and companioned by Hagar. I trusted her—was certain that a well or a divine messenger (or both) would appear, that everything my daughters and I needed would be provided, that even if it were not, we would survive. Hagar walked with me through every day, every sleepless night, every dark chapter of my story and life, reminding me that I was seen, heard, and honored. She does, still.

———— ❦ ————

HAGAR WAS AN ENSLAVED WOMAN with no resources, no family, nothing and no one on whom she could depend. Her decision to run could have easily ended her life and her child's. She left anyway. It wasn't really a choice. *She knew.*

And she knows, even now, even still. . . .

Of all the wisdom she longs to offer us, all that she wants us to believe and trust, her voice rings out, again and again, saying, "You already know."

You already know that it's time to walk away. *You already know* that the relationship is over. *You already know* that you are compromising yourself. *You already know* that the hard conversations ahead are going to be yours to start and finish. *You already know* that your job is not a fit. *You already know* that you have to leave the church. *You already know* that what you once believed and trusted in isn't working anymore. *You already know* that your perspective and opinion matter. *You already know* that you are more than enough and deserve the best. You *already know. You already know. You already know.*

But not alone. Never alone.

Hagar *already knows* of our every what-if and worry. She knows we wish and wait for validation and encouragement, for someone else to step up. She knows we secretly pray for a miracle, an intervention, the ability to endure a bit longer. She knows that the beauty and strength of our knowing is not remotely contingent on whether we follow through on it—or don't. She knows we deserve grace. She knows that our intuition and wisdom can be trusted. She knows there is no reason to doubt our capacity, our courage, even our wobbly next steps. And she knows we will one day believe her when we hear her say, "You already know."

You should know that I have questioned all of this more times than I can count. I have anxiously listed out all the things that could possibly go wrong if I actually believed her and/or believed in myself. I have swirled and obsessed and created pro-and-con lists and prayed and bargained and lived in massive denial. I have poured more wine and watched more TV. I have moved furniture and cleaned closets and shopped online. Once, while still married, I completely repainted and redecorated our bedroom, convinced that a change in the environment would change everything else as well, even though *I already knew*. It was just so much easier to pretend that I didn't.

Hagar's story brings me back from pretending in a heartbeat. In my most desperate moments, even in my best ones, she is who I look to and lean on. *I already know* that she knows everything I am feeling and fearing. *I already know* that she is here and I am not alone, ever. *I already know* what she will tell me. Somehow, hearing it from her—a woman who knew unfathomable trauma and terror, who chose to stand her ground and save her own life, who was met by divine messengers and miracles and blessings untold—offers me the exact consolation I need and compels my courage. I stand a bit taller. I feel *worth* saving. I let myself consider the possibility that even though it all looks impossible right now, perhaps I, too, will know divine messengers and miracles and blessings. And I admit that she's been right all along: *I DO already know.*

As do you.

But on days when you forget, when you feel forsaken and forlorn, when miles and miles of sand are all that appear to stretch before you, Hagar offers you her hand, her certainty, her confidence, and *her knowing* on your behalf. Like water in the desert.

IN ONE OF OUR FIRST SESSIONS TOGETHER, my spiritual director asked, "Ronna, how would you describe God?"

I gave her all the expected responses: *in control of the arc of history, faithful and trustworthy, has a plan that is far bigger than what I can possibly see or understand, immutable and inviolate and incarnate.*

Check. Check. Check.

After a few more poignant questions (and some less-than-subtle direction), I tentatively began to describe the god I *actually* knew, the one that more often sounded like *you'd better get it right* and *be good if you want my love* and *you'll never be good enough or worthy enough* and *I'll listen, but only if you're perfect.* It shocked me to acknowledge any of this at all, let alone out loud. I had never admitted such doubt or frustration—not to myself, not to someone else. Every sentence left me feeling confused and ashamed. After all, I had grown up in the church, gone to a Christian college, worked for a missionary organization, was a pastor's wife, and was in the process of pursuing my Master of Divinity degree! But revealed that day, beneath a highly polished exterior and burdensome expectations, was a glimpse of something raw, honest, and true. I named my *experience* instead of offering the right answers. I spoke of a god who I felt had ignored me, who had not listened to my cries. In my confusing teenage years, as I flailed through my twenties, as I suffered through infertility in my thirties, or now, in my forties, as I endured a painful marriage. This god was distant, seemingly deaf, judgmental, passive (and sometimes aggressive), aloof, untouchable, inanimate. And though all of this made me feel angry and angsty, I was relatively certain, even in the moment, that naming any of this was evidence of *my* mistake, *my* fault, *my* lack of faith—was clearly mine to recant and repent.

A few months later, she asked how I would describe Hagar's god.

This god intentionally found, appeared, and spoke with a woman who was completely marginalized, even invisible. This god made vast promises to a woman with no status or rights—one who would not have believed in the divine in the first place or dared to hope in such. This god chose her—no demands or expectations, just kindness and grace and blessing. This god appeared in the desert—in the heat and desolation and endlessness of it all. This god showed up for her; she was not alone.

"Did that god's presence depend upon her good behavior or unswerving belief?"

No.

"Is it possible that maybe, just maybe, *that god* sees you in your desert, Ronna? That maybe, just maybe, *that god* does not require your perfection, your martyrdom, or any more of your suffering? Could it be that the divine shows up for you? Could it be that you're not alone either?"

Maybe.

"Mmmm. That feels significant, yes?"

Yes.

———— ⟨⟩ ————

THEOPHANY IS A THEOLOGICAL TERM FOR the appearance of God, the manifestation of a deity in visible form. There are more than fifty theophanies in the bible, including a burning bush, a wrestling man, a commander with a sword, and an angel who appears to a young pregnant woman and says, "Do not be afraid." But the very first of them all? The very first time the divine is *ever* seen?

Hagar saw God before anyone else.

A *woman* saw God before anyone else.

God chose to be seen by a woman, by Hagar, before anyone else.

If this weren't shocking and amazing enough, all that we might attribute to being "worthy" of such an honor is completely turned upside down in her story. God chose to be seen *first* by a woman who was enslaved, in exile, marginalized, abused, pregnant, and completely alone in the desert. In her book *Womanist Midrash*, Wilda C. Gafney says, "This is extraordinary, for Exodus 33:20 will insist that no one can see God and live; perhaps those verses ought to be translated as 'no *man*.' "⁴ Despite how many years I have spent researching the blatant and heart-wrenching lack of attention and care paid to women in this text, it still shocks me that *no one ever talks about this!*

Countless volumes have told us more than we ever wanted to know about Eve—a woman blamed for casting the world into an endless pit of despair—but few to none tell of the woman to and for whom the divine showed up first and literally. Had we heralded this truth and Hagar herself, the realities women have had to bear for generations and still today would be anathema. Had we known a god who is intentionally present on a woman's behalf, none of us would have had to wrestle with and/or walk away from a faith that contradicts our value and worth at nearly every turn. Had we acknowledged that it is in the desert—the most barren of circumstances—that the divine is visibly and repeatedly present for women, we would have risked any number of "leavings" far sooner, assured that we would not be alone, that we would be seen and heard, that we would be honored and blessed.

Maybe it's not too late.

Hagar's theophany is not her only distinction. In Genesis 15, God says to Abraham, "Look up at the sky and count the stars, if indeed you can count them. So shall your offspring be." Then, just verses later, in chapter 16, God says to Hagar, "I will increase your descendants so much that they will be too numerous to count." The esteemed patriarch within the trifecta of the Abrahamic religions (Christianity, Judaism, Islam) is *not* the sole recipient of the divine's blessing and favor; the very same belongs to a woman, to Hagar. We have (intentionally, it seems) neglected to name the fact that the very woman the patriarch disregarded, even harmed, was given the exact same promise as her perpetrator—by a god who blatantly overturned all misguided interpretations of patriarchal precedence or preference.

Had we learned of a god who loved a woman so much that she was promised *exactly* as much as was promised to a man—not just any man but the patriarch himself—we would never have accepted anything less in roles, responsibilities, or relationships. Had we known of a god who *undoes* patriarchy vs. supports and strengthens it, we would have freed ourselves long ago from its flimsy argument about "god's will" or "divine intention." Had we heard about a god who immediately sees a woman's pain, hears her distress, and then answers with blessing and hope, we would have never given allegiance to the one (so we've been told) who promises to save us only when and if we are good enough.

Maybe it's not too late.

Hagar holds a third distinction as well: she is the first and *only* person in the Hebrew bible to give God a name. The only person. A woman. This woman—enslaved, in exile, marginalized, abused, pregnant, and completely alone in the desert—names God *El Roi*, which means "I have seen the One who sees me."

I have seen the One who sees me. Hagar is the subject and the object. She is the one around whom this definition of the divine swirls—an understanding of the divine that cannot exist without her. She is the one who is seen. She is the one who sees. A woman. This woman. Lost. Afraid. Desolate. And *almost* alone, but for the child in her womb and a god who will not leave her side.

Had this been the god of whom we'd been told, by whom we'd been comforted, with whom we'd walked, whom we'd seen and who had seen us—*really* seen us—we would never have doubted our value and worth. And we would have been in relationship with a god who is far different from the male one of which we've learned. A *woman's* god—a god who shows up and is seen, a god who blesses, a god we name as we see fit, based on our experience of dancing with the divine in the desert.

Maybe it's not too late.

Now that we know? Now that we've heard? Now that we've seen? Now that *we* are known, heard, and seen? It changes *everything*.

Admittedly, it is hard to dare imagine a god like Hagar's. Especially if we've walked (or run) away from the god we were taught and told to believe in. Especially if we've been betrayed by that god and the religion, the institution of the church, and those who protect it at any cost. Especially if we've known violence and harm—a lack of compassion and care from the very people and institutions who should have been providing it without measure. After all this, to open ourselves to this kind of belief can feel daunting, if not foolish; but it's never too late . . .

Hagar and her god invite us to cherish the sacred in new ways—distinctly feminine, released from doctrine and dogma—to wander freely in a vast spiritual landscape that is uniquely and powerfully our own. Hagar and her god remind us to see ourselves as not only worthy of but *specifically chosen* for divine intentionality, promise, and intimate care. Hagar and her god compel us to decry, yet again, the lies of "not enough" or "too much." Hagar and her god empower us to know—despite every story we've been told—that *all* women, past-present-future, are heard, seen, advocated for, honored, and blessed by birthright and divine decree.

Mmmmm. That feels significant, yes?

IT WOULD BE LOVELY IF HAGAR'S STORY came to a close with an extravagant god and endless blessing—her personal version of "happily ever after." But it doesn't end that way at all. In truth, the "ending" of her story is confusing, unresolved, and painful. Just like mine.

It was excruciating to tell my daughters that their dad would no longer be living with us. Our goodbyes on the Friday mornings that signaled a weekend apart were brutal. It was harder still to welcome them back home and listen to them cry, hold them tight, and promise it wouldn't always feel this way. It broke my heart when they asked why I had to go to work, why they had to go to daycare, why I couldn't see how much easier it would be if Dad came back home. It was all I could do to keep it together. And let's be clear: I *did not* keep it together. More days than not, for a very long time, I felt lost. I was no longer the pastor's wife, a woman who repeated Romans 8:28[5] and oh-so-efficiently pushed down my grief and rage. I would not return—despite moments in which I desperately wished I could—to the well-rehearsed platitudes of my faith. I was in the desert with no happily-ever-after in sight. Even now, sixteen-plus years later, I still feel the sand in my shoes.

The most excruciating part of Hagar's story is when she is told to go back to Sarai and Abram—back to her enslavement, back to the place of her abuse and her abusers. It has the capacity to unravel everything good and gracious we've come to see and understand thus far. I could tell you of how this has been interpreted through-out time, how it's been used to force women's return to abusive husbands and marriages, how it's been justified by claiming the common law of the time—the practice of returning enslaved people to their "masters"—how it's been made supposedly less offensive by interpreting it as a metaphor for Israel's relationship with their god. But even if I could land on something, anything, that makes sense, it wouldn't change the reality of Hagar's story or the god who required her return.

There's no making sense of it as long as we demand a story that does. And perhaps that is the point. When we tell Hagar's story as it is, we cannot ignore her harm and abuse. It requires that we boldly and blatantly name what is *not* acceptable. It compels us to honestly acknowledge the pain that women distinctly know—always have. It forces an end to any blatant or subtle justification of such pain. When we make excuses or explanations, skip over the parts we don't like, or apply a patina of cultural norms, Hagar's story becomes dull and increasingly irrelevant. Saddest of all, we lose any way of finding ourselves within it.

Her story makes us cringe; we bristle at all that is irreconcilable in her world and therefore our own. Which requires that we, too, return—to the thick of things, to injustices, to the contradictions and paradoxes and conflicts we witness and experience both individually and collectively. Not a happy ending, but certainly a real one. Not with acceptance or compliance, but with defiance and determination. Were Hagar's story to conclude with an end to all her pain and an answer to all her prayers, we would be left with one more fairy tale in our collection; we would feel exactly as we have all along—alone, unseen, and unheard. Instead, her story offers us just the opposite.

As does her god.

———— ❦ ————

JUST AFTER HAGAR HAS BEEN TOLD TO return to everything she's justifiably run away from, the divine messenger says this: "You will give birth to a son. Name him Ishmael, for the Lord has heard of your misery. He will be a wild ass of a man, his hand will be against everyone, and everyone's hand will be against him. He will live in hostility toward all his brothers." (Genesis 16:12)

At first glance, this would appear as adding insult to injury: pregnant by force, abused by the woman who demanded it, forsaken and alone in the desert, and promised a son who will be a "wild ass of a man." But when we look closer, this is profound gift and grace. Hagar could not have asked for a greater promise on her son's behalf! It gave her the certainty that her fate would not continue for another generation. She was assured that Ishmael would *not* be restrained at all—that he would be free. He would fight against domestication, against service to a master, against anyone or anything that would attempt to tame him. He would be wild!

Hagar's story, when rewritten, reimagined, and redeemed, is a missing link in our own evolution and development. It unravels the centuries-old tale of women as domesticated, living to serve, and painfully and perfectly tamed. The blessing Hagar receives on behalf of her son is, in fact, the blessing we have needed all along. *Be wild. It is your destiny, your birthright, your truest expression. Nothing less will do.*

Tragically, we have not been given much opportunity to even consider our "wildness" as blessing. In nearly every aspect of our lives, such a thing is more often attributed to curse. Any hint at being uninhibited, unbridled, outrageous, or free and seemingly out of control is quickly shut down, shunned, or shamed—most likely, all three in short order. We have unwittingly become the opposite of wild.

Be a lady. Keep your shit together. Keep the peace. Mind your manners. Calm down. Stay in control. Every one of these external demands domesticate the wild right out of us. And in time, we forget who we are and that we were always meant to be free. We're like the story told of elephants who are tied by a small rope at a very young age. As they grow, they are conditioned to not break away so that as adults, though far stronger than the rope that holds them, they never attempt to break free. We don't realize that we can leave, that we can return home.

Be wild. It is your destiny, your birthright, your truest expression. Nothing less will do.

Though "wild" looks and feels unique and original to each of us, it is a consistent and powerful force that we share: untethered and creative, instinctual and expansive, unbridled and fierce. It waits to be breathed back into being, to bless as intended, to be remembered. As Clarissa Pinkola Estés describes it, "The memory is of our absolute, undeniable, and irrevocable kinship with the wild feminine, a relationship which may have become ghosty with neglect, buried by over-domestication, outlawed by the surrounding culture, or no longer understood anymore. We may have forgotten her names, we may not answer when she calls, but in our bones we know her, we yearn toward her; we know she belongs to us and we to her."[6]

"Wild" can also be defined by our reaction and response to anything that *limits* our rightful and promised freedom. Harm. Abuse. Disrespect. Unequal treatment. Misogyny. Demands that contort. Ties that bind. Beliefs that restrict. Sacred texts that silence or shame. Any assertion that we are not enough or too much. Our wildness is a rejection of this—for ourselves and for others. It is boldly, even defiantly, demanding our place, our value, and our worth.

Wild. Untamed. Unrestrained. Alive. Awake. Passionate. Bold. Free. Though nearly every one of these aspects of "womanhood" have been taken from us, even demonized, we know better. And when Hagar's story is reimagined, we recall, deep within and at last, that we are worthy recipients of her endless blessing on our behalf: *Be wild. It is your destiny, your birthright, your truest expression. Nothing less will do.*

———— ❦ ————

I WISH I HAD GROWN UP RELYING ON the voice within me that says, "*You already know.*" I wish I had repeatedly and confidently applied Hagar's wisdom in relationships, jobs, even self-talk, instead of endlessly compromising and complying. I wish my wildness had been affirmed, that I had expressed it no matter what. I wish that I had chosen "entirely out of control" over the *many* times I bit my tongue, buried my emotions, ignored my intuition, played the part, crossed my fingers, and hoped for the best. I wish I had done a better job of inviting and encouraging every one of Hagar's traits and characteristics in my daughters. I wish I had more years left to experience *her* experience of the divine. I wish I could live to see Hagar as a beautiful and defiant model of what it means to be a woman in this world—of all the things for which we *should* be honored: our insistence upon justice, our endless courage, our defiant voice, our wild giftedness, and our worthiness of receiving divine presence and promise.

For all that I wish, gratitude pervades. I am eternally grateful for those earliest days in front of my computer as I tentatively began to imagine Hagar's voice, experience her presence, and witness her god. And I am forever grateful for the strength she gave me, the companionship she provided, the tears she witnessed, the perseverance she compelled, and the unending compassion she showed me. I am grateful for the endless deserts she walked with me—that she walks with me still.

More than all else, I hope. I hope you will fall in love with Hagar as I have, that you will let her love you in return. I hope you will hear her voice on your behalf even now. I hope you will believe her when she says, "*You already know.*" I hope you will find solace and strength in a god who defies everything you've been told. I hope you will answer her call to *your* wildness. I hope in your deserts—which surely will come—you will let her take your hand, walk with you, and endlessly remind you that you are her daughter, her lineage, her kin.

Dear One:

You are not lost or alone. I have been with you all along—in every grain of this arid terrain, every moment of desolation, every bit of this torturing heat. I have been the solid ground and certainty within you decrying every mirage—structure and safety, staying within the lines, following the rules, not daring to raise your voice to anything that leaves you feeling less-than.

Gratefully and finally, all of that has now been left behind. There are no lines, no boundaries, no borders. The rules are yours to create. It is time to raise your voice and say, "enough"—to be the wild and untamed woman that has always been intended, has always been yours for the taking. Nothing to second-guess or regret.

Now, with your hand in mine, we will walk together. We will partake of the divine's radical blessing on our behalf: water and wildness and life beyond anything we can imagine. Nothing less will do for you—my daughter, my lineage, my kin.

QUESTIONS FOR
FURTHER REFLECTION:

1. What is your response to Hagar's voice on your behalf when she says, "You already know"?

2. The risks inherent in Hagar's decision to run away were vast. She ran anyway. What grace does she extend to you for the times when you couldn't run, when the costs felt too much and the risks too high?

3. Hagar encounters a god that is far different than the one of whom we've been told. When you acknowledge what you have come to believe about the divine, what is missing, broken, confusing, or maybe even wrong? What do you *want* to believe? How would encountering Hagar's god impact you?

4. What do you make of the fact that little has ever been said about Hagar being the very first person to see the divine?

5. Think of your own desert experiences—the places of harm, relationships, situations, or jobs from which you've run. Now, picture Hagar alongside you in every one. What if you weren't alone even then? What if you are not alone even now?

6. *Were Hagar's story to conclude with an end to all her pain and an answer to all her prayers, we would be left with one more fairy tale in our collection. . . .* How do you respond to this? What is the benefit of having stories that are far from perfect as a source of encouragement and strength?

7. What would be different if you chose to be wild and untamed? What would be different if you already believed that you are?

Chapter Four: THE MIDWIVES

Women helped each other in ways small and large every day, without thinking, and that was what kept them going even when the world came up with new and exciting ways to crush them.

—ALYSSA COLE

I did not have a midwife for either of my daughters' births. Instead of intentional warmth, nurture, and encouragement, I experienced a sterile distance, bright lights, *lots* of staff bustling around the room, a male doctor who rushed in at the *very* last possible minute, even a male lactation consultant. I wouldn't trade a millisecond of those memories; still, I sometimes imagine what it would have been like to be companioned by another woman through two of the most significant experiences of my life. A woman who was there for the express purpose of providing me support, who called forth my capacity, who advocated on my behalf and that of my child; a woman who was nonplussed by my emotions, my pain, or my fear; a woman who would stay with me no matter what.

This applies far above and beyond the experience of pregnancy, labor, and delivery. The constant and committed companionship, support, advocacy, and presence of other women is something all women desire and deserve in every moment of life. Most of us, though, struggle to know what this looks or feels like. We've had very little modeling, very few examples, even fewer stories told.

Virginia Woolf said, "I tried to remember any case in the course of my reading where two women are represented as friends. . . . But almost without exception they are shown in their relation to men. . . . And how a small part of a woman's life is that."[1]

The story of the Midwives *is* an exception . . . and exceptional. These two women have so much to teach, to offer, and to help us birth into the world.

Their Text
—paraphrased from Exodus, chapter 1

Generations passed after Hagar's story. Over the next seven hundred years, the Israelite people became the "great nation" that had been foretold. But as would be the case multiple times in their history, they eventually found themselves in captivity—this time in Egypt.

Despite hardship and suffering, they were "exceedingly fruitful" and grew in number. This was *not* what the Pharaoh wanted to hear. He said, "Look, the Israelites have become far too numerous for us. We must do something before things get worse; if war breaks out, they will join our enemies, fight against us, and leave." So, he put slave masters over them and oppressed them even more. But it didn't matter: the worse things got, the more they multiplied. The Egyptians came to dread the Israelites and treated them more and more ruthlessly as time went on.

In desperate response to this situation, the Pharaoh called two midwives, Shiphrah and Puah, into his presence. "When you are helping the Hebrew women during childbirth," he instructed them, "kill any boy and let the girls live." But instead of doing what they were commanded, the midwives helped birth girls and boys alike. When he learned of their failure to comply, again the Pharaoh summoned them into his presence. "Why have you done this?" he demanded. "Why have you let the boys live?" They answered him, "Hebrew women are not like Egyptian women; they are vigorous and give birth before we can even arrive."

The text tells us that God was kind to the midwives and gave them families of their own. Meanwhile, the Israelite people continued to increase. The Pharaoh, even more enraged, sent down a decree to all his people: "Every Hebrew boy that is born you must throw into the Nile but let every girl live."

———— ❦ ————

The story of the Midwives is stunningly beautiful, movie-worthy—the stuff of literature and poetry, even song. Yet these two women remain relatively unknown and have too often been overshadowed by the epic story of Moses—the text they immediately precede and, quite frankly, make possible. An infant boy who was *not* killed at birth but instead put in a basket of reeds and floated down the river. A baby rescued by the Pharaoh's daughter and raised as royalty who grew into a man who led the Israelites' escape from slavery, through the Red Sea, and eventually into the Promised Land. It's an amazing tale. But as long as the patriarch holds our collective gaze, women are slighted; they are not honored or esteemed as they deserve. *We* are slighted. We have little to go on when it comes to women's friendship. We are not gifted with the awareness and certainty that everything changes when we support and love each other.

We are far more familiar with the opposite: cattiness, competition, shifting loyalties, distrust—all glamorized by "good" reality TV. Scene after scene. Battle after battle. A fight over a man. A stolen partner or husband. Horrible female bosses. Stepmothers who ignore or harm. Mothers who wound or leave. When not balanced by beautiful *and true* stories of women's friendship, support, and love, we start to believe the rhetoric: Women can't be trusted. Women are manipulative. Women don't help women. On and on it goes . . . all the way back to Eve (or so we've been told).

We desperately need the story of the Midwives rescued and reimagined. A picture of what it looks like to be present on each other's behalf in pain *and* celebration, bleeding *and* birth, pushing *and* resisting. A model of endlessly reminding each other to breathe. A witnessing of their willingness to face tremendous risk because of the courage they found in each other. A way to see that they are capable of bravely companioning and consoling us because of their fierce advocacy for each other. A poignant and powerful reminder that women are the most important people in our lives, that we need not go it alone.

———— ⊂⊃≋⊂⊃ ————

I HAVEN'T ALWAYS HAD FRIENDSHIPS with women in deep and *change-everything* ways. I haven't always known how to allow them close enough to see my emotions, my pain, or my fear. It took me a while to realize the myriad of ways in which women strengthen me, support me, and enable me to step into so much more of the life that is mine. Surprisingly, I learned at least the beginnings of this not from the Midwives but from my dad.

When I was twenty years old and a junior in college, I rarely ventured out of my dorm room other than for class, work, and a quick walk to the Student Union Building for my dinner, which most often consisted of a frozen Snickers bar, Cheetos, and a Tab. This instead of facing the dining hall and my fear that I'd eat alone, surrounded by people who were not.

My dad stopped by for a visit one Sunday afternoon. He sat on the edge of my bed and asked me how I was doing. For some reason, instead of feigning confidence and telling him everything was fine, I answered honestly. I told him I was lonely, that I didn't feel like I had any friends, that I was isolated and isolating. I can still hear his response like it was yesterday:

"Ronna Jo. What do you think people see when you walk across campus?"

"I don't know what you mean."

"Do they see a young woman who moves deliberately and confidently, who knows where she is going, who is obviously focused and determined, who appears to have everything in control?"

"Probably."

"So how would anyone know what you are feeling? How would anyone know that you need them? You have to let people in, be vulnerable, *ask* for others' support, time, even friendship."

"But how? No one wants to deal with my sadness or insecurity. That's too much to ask."

"I think you're wrong about that; if the tables were turned, you'd be supportive, generous, and kind. But for the sake of the argument, let's test it out. Is there someone, even right here in your dorm, that you'd like to get to know better? Could you just write her a note and slip it under her door? Invite her out for coffee or meet her for lunch? Just one small step?"

The two of us probably talked longer, but that's all I remember. Well, except for this: later that week I *did* write the note and slip it under her door. It didn't feel like a small step at all; rather, it felt like a giant and incredibly risky mistake. I was certain she'd pretend to have never received it. Even when she enthusiastically said yes, I was pretty sure it was out of pity, not mutual interest.

In spite of myself, we became friends.

I imagine the Midwives smiled knowingly at each other while my dad spoke. I imagine they walked by my side as I took his advice and risked the smallest of steps. I imagine they excitedly grasped each other's hands every time I reluctantly ventured outside my safe-but-lonely world. I imagine that when I've felt most alone at any time in my life, they have conspired to send the perfect woman my way: a colleague, a mentor, a muse, my sister, my daughters, a Jesuit nun, the dearest of friends, and every single one of these ancient, sacred stories and women that have companioned me beyond belief.

Far more than imagine, I *believe* this is exactly what the story of the Midwives generously offers on our behalf. They remind us of what is *more* true, *more* generous, and *more* empowering than what we've been told, what we've witnessed, even what we may have been through. Their courage catalyzes and compels our own. Their example enables us to change everything as they did: one brave act at a time, one life at a time, and together.

Would the profound legacy of the Midwives have been possible, let alone told, if there had been only one of them? Would either Shiphrah or Puah, by herself, have had the strength to resist the Pharaoh, to think with such cunning under pressure, to give such a creative and even witty response about the Hebrew women being "more vigorous" than Egyptian women and giving birth before she could get there? Maybe. But that is not the story we have been told. Thankfully. Nor is it the one we are called to live.

From that earliest of lessons via my dad and so many that have followed, I have learned that the more I reveal my needs and desires, the more they are met. The more I let myself be seen in honest, open-hearted ways instead of self-protective and misguided ones, the more I am known and loved. The more I ask of others, the more I receive—and the more I have to give. The women I have befriended, respected, and known have strengthened and enhanced how I see myself in the world, how I experience my own power, and how I show up in my own story. A far cry from that day in my dorm. Thankfully.

———— ⟨⟐⟩ ————

NOT ALL THAT LONG AGO, I HELD A SENIOR leadership position in "corporate America." For the first year, I worked for and alongside other women. Every bit of the experience was fabulous. We created. We collaborated. We labored. We laughed. We struggled. We celebrated. Then almost overnight, things changed, and I found myself working for a man. It was no longer fabulous. Before six months had passed, I left.

To be fair, there *were* extenuating circumstances above/beyond issues of gender (like a pandemic). I don't exclusively mean to say that this is most often the way of it—though in my own career this *has*, sadly, been the case more often than not.

My point, however, is not about the men I've worked *for* but rather about the women I've had the privilege of working *with*.

Something powerful, alchemical, even magical occurs when women stand alongside each other, create and build together, imagine and strategize and compel both individual and collective success. And this is hardly limited to corporate environments; it is just as true in volunteer contexts, for parents involved in their kid's school, for entrepreneurial ventures, in coaching, therapy, and mentorship relationships—the list goes on and on. And though I've heard stories of women competing, climbing, and stepping on and over the top of one another in all kinds of pursuits, that has not been my personal experience. Just the opposite.

We need more of this—more of each other, more relationships with women that support and encourage. We need to trust and know that we are not heading into the fray alone, that the risks we take are a necessary embodiment of the values and beliefs we share, that we stand and potentially fall, but always with each other. We need to trust that we are exponentially stronger and far more capable of changing *everything* when we have each other's back, when we cheer one another on, when we combine forces for good. It is the "how" that often eludes us.

And once again, the Midwives come alongside. They serve as the most powerful of metaphors, the most powerful of teachers.

A midwife is present in a time of vulnerability. She is a teacher who helps the birthgiver toward ever-greater self-knowledge. She knows when the birthgiver should push and when to hold back. She can hear, ask, and even demand the seemingly impossible. And she can rejoice in and celebrate the beauty and absurdity of new and amazing life.[2]

We don't do this for each other perfectly or consistently, of course. But even as we falter and sometimes fail, we experience the profound offering of grace that women uniquely provide. I have experienced this more times than I can count—women who have held my hand, wiped my brow, talked sense into me, consistently seen me more clearly than I could see myself, and celebrated wildly when I demonstrated the strength and courage they always knew I had. They have midwifed me into who I am today. And thankfully, graciously, they teach me, over and over again, to offer the same to others.

Then there are the ancient, sacred women themselves. Like a great cloud of witnesses, they have encircled me, held me close, lifted me up, dried my tears, believed in my inherent worthiness, and stayed and stayed and stayed. Eve. Cain's Wife. Hagar. The Midwives. And so many more. Just as real, just as close, just as present.

The women I have known personally and the women whose stories I tell have changed everything for and about me. And they have made one thing endlessly and abundantly clear: No matter what, *I am not alone.*

And neither are you.

———— ❦ ————

IN HER BOOK *HIDDEN FIGURES*, Margot Lee Shetterly tells the true story of three Black female mathematicians at NASA whose calculations helped fuel some of America's greatest achievements in space. In an interview, she said:

> History is the sum total of what all of us do on a daily basis. We think of capital "H" history as being these huge figures—George Washington, Alexander Hamilton, and Martin Luther King. Even so, you go to bed at night, you wake up the next morning, and then yesterday is history. These small actions in some ways are more important or certainly as important as the individual actions by these towering figures.[3]

Generations of women, the Midwives among them, have gone to bed at night and woken up the next morning. They have birthed life into the world in every form. They have sustained and saved life in infinite ways. They have survived life itself. Each of these are "certainly as important as the individual actions by towering figures."

Andrée de Jongh saved hundreds of Allied airmen escaping from the Nazis, and Freddie and Truus Oversteegen spent their teenage years luring Nazis to their death by seducing them. Frances Perkins was the first woman to serve on the US Cabinet. Aung San Suu Kyi spent fifteen years on house arrest in the name of non-violence and democracy. Roberta "Bobbi" Gibb ran in the Boston Marathon after being rejected because she was a woman. Amani Al-Khatahtbeh started a pioneering publication by and for Muslim women. Rosalind Franklin discovered the double helix structure of DNA. Sybil Ludington rode twice as far as Paul Revere to warn about the British. Mary McLeod Bethune served on FDR's "Black Cabinet" working as an activist for education and civil rights. Lee Miller spent years photographing all the heroic women of World War II. Gertrude Bell was a legendary explorer who helped establish modern day Iraq.[4]

We rarely, if ever, hear of these "small actions"—these day-in, day-out efforts of women who profoundly shape the world in which we live. Because were we to do so—were we to know, affirm, and perpetuate the legacy that is ours—it would completely upset the patriarchal equilibrium and break the cultural rules that are designed and enforced to keep us in our place. Every one of these stories, including the Midwives and including our own, deserves to be heard; every "small action" that makes up a woman's life and that, along the way, has the power to change everything deserves to be known.

But if we're completely honest, we must admit that it is this, exactly, that we both hope for and fear at the very same time. To change everything can be—is—incredibly risky. We *know* the impact of our story when told and lived in out loud, even non-compliant, ways. We will, to be sure, upset the equilibrium and break the rules. And we *know* what this can cost. . . .

When we say no to anything that compromises us or others.

When we choose courage over compliance.

When we risk everything on behalf of what we know to be right and true.

When we listen and respond to the cries of labor around us— all that deserves to be birthed and nurtured.

When we refuse to let our boundaries be breached yet again.

When we love who we love—regardless of laws or opinions.

When we do the hard and ongoing work of acknowledging our own internalized racism.

When we demonstrate, lobby, and vote on behalf of women's right to their own bodies, their very choices.

When we speak up in a meeting at work even though doing so goes against the grain.

When we refuse to internalize patriarchal messages that intentionally have us doubting whether or not we are enough.

When we do not believe the overculture that tells us we only matter when we are young and beautiful (and that we must endlessly strive toward and purchase such).

When we stand humbly alongside other women, other humans, who have known harm, violence, bigotry, and bias that we cannot begin to imagine.

When we refuse relationships that require our silence or perpetuate our shame.

It is understandable that we would feel overwhelmed, tentative, and afraid. There is so much power to defy, so much injustice to refuse, so much in our own life to heal, restore, and redeem; there are so many generations to save. So, when we hear a story like that of the Midwives, we are inspired *and* we wonder how they had the courage to do what they did.

Though I don't know for sure, I can make an informed guess: They did exactly what you have done and will do yet again. Get up in the morning. Take the next step. Go to sleep at night. Take risks. Say no. Stand tall, side by side with others. Stand up to the powers that be. Make history. And abandon any story that tries to convince you that you are alone.

Instead, remember, reimagine, and follow the lead of a story that affirms what has always been true: you are the Midwives' daughter, their lineage, their kin.

———————— ❦ ————————

MERLIN STONE FAMOUSLY WROTE, "At the very dawn of religion, God was a woman. Do you remember?"[5] Legend, lore, myth, and certainly archeological evidence reveal that cultures far predating Christianity revered women gods— deified and honored our cycles, our blood, our ability to bring forth life. History has revealed that the fear of these very things is what ultimately compelled and sustained men's need to exert domination and control—a perspective already solidified by the time the very first story in scripture was told. The feminine was erased from our understanding and experience of the sacred, even from our experience of each other and ourselves.

In the words of Rebecca Solnit: "Some women get erased a little at a time, some all at once. Some reappear. Every woman who appears wrestles with the forces that would have her disappear. She struggles with the forces that would tell her story for her, or write her out of the story, the genealogy, the rights of man, the rule of law. The ability to tell your own story, in words or images, is already a victory, already a revolt."[6]

To reimagine the story of the Midwives is a revolt—a revolutionary return to the undeniable power of the feminine. We remember what is actually true: the pharaoh did *not* win, the Midwives did *not* fail, deliverance and redemption *did* occur because of two brave women. And we remember what is actually true about our own brave stories: every "birth" we assist and those we create and bear ourselves, every page we write and song we sing and diaper we change and tear we shed and meal we prepare and conference table we command and team we lead; every woman we honor, support, and befriend; every "pharaoh" we defy; every miracle we bring forth by *being* the miracles we are. We are *not* erased. We *are* the feminine—the sacred feminine embodied and enfleshed. Remember?

TRADITIONALLY, MIDWIVES DID NOT have children of their own. Without family responsibilities, they were available at all hours for everyone else. What was it like for them—night after night, week after week, month after month, and year after year—to help other women birth children into the world but not know the same for themselves? Somehow, despite the excruciating and ongoing reminder of their own barrenness, they brought forth the very life that eluded them. I do not know how they did it.

I spent five years hoping for a child, doing everything in my (and modern science's) power to have one, and praying-then-weeping every twenty-eight days at my failure to conceive. My heart shattered each time I saw an infant in a stroller or a toddler holding their parent's hand. And Mother's Day? *Aaaaaaugh.* It was endless: my anger, disappointment, grief, rage, betrayal, self-contempt, and shame. But I expressed little to none of it. No one knew how much I hurt. I barely acknowledged it to myself.

Looking back, I can extend myself at least a modicum of grace for my lack of expressed emotion given the religious milieu I was in at the time: the pastor's wife, expected to keep my spirits up and belief intact, a model of what it looked like to hold fast to God's faithfulness on my behalf, no matter my circumstances. Even if I'd not experienced the external pressure, I felt every bit of it internally. I had learned to believe in a god who had a perfect plan for my life. I quoted the verse engraved inside my wedding ring: *For I know the plans I have for you, declares the Lord; plans to prosper you and not to harm you. Plans to give you a future and a hope* (Jeremiah 29:11). I clung to any and everything that offered me "proof" that my prayers would eventually work, that God would eventually listen, that a miracle would eventually occur. And so, when yet another round of IUI failed, when the tests showed no elevated HCG levels, when I felt the familiar return of blood, I both drifted in a sea of internal tumult *and* kept a death grip on the precepts that had promised to sustain me. I never considered the possibility that I could believe *and* be filled with rage, that I could be devoted *and* know desolation, that there was even the remotest possibility of a god who could handle and hold every bit of that, every bit of me. Instead, afraid of risking God's disfavor, I shoved my feelings down, journaled privately (with exhausting restraint), sobbed in private, and forced myself to hold fast to a divine plan in which "God's ways are higher than ours," not mine to know or understand.

I have often wondered what my own experience of infertility would have been like had it not been complicated by my from-the-womb understanding of the divine. If it would have been more healing (and certainly more freeing) to express my pain and longing when not conflicted by the axiom of "pray without ceasing." If I might have found far more solace, even relief, if not constrained by the need to remain faith-full.

Now, and repeatedly, I *do* grieve. For the losses I silenced too many times. For the woman I once was—so afraid that my honesty would be my undoing, not only related to infertility but in nearly every other aspect of my life. For the women I have known who weep, whose arms are empty, whose wombs hold unmeasurable ache. For a world that does not prioritize or esteem women's reproductive health. For not having been shown the Midwives as a template for how to celebrate *and* grieve, give *and* want, enable life *and* know its lack.

As you know, I have two daughters. When I found out that I was pregnant with Emma Joy, I took seven at-home pregnancy tests, unable to believe any of them. It was only when a doctor confirmed what every pink line had already named that I finally was convinced. As you might guess, I endlessly expressed my thanks to God, certain that "He" had enabled such a miracle. And every bit of this was repeated two years later when Abby Evangeline came into the world.

Today, I do *not* believe that my blind obedience and dogged determination to remain faithful to God was what brought them into being—as though I somehow finally did enough to deserve them. Nor do I ever want to think that had I *not* conceived, *not* given birth, that it was the inevitable outcome of my lack of obedience or devotion.

At the end of their story, we are told that God gave the Midwives children of their own. It is easy to use this as proof-text—evidence that if we just endure, "keep the faith," and suffer in silence, God will come through. Missing in that simplistic explanation, however, is that these two women did *not* serve the Hebrew god. As Egyptians, they likely worshiped goddesses, practiced magic, and engaged in ritual to enable their own fertility *and* that of the Hebrew women they served. So, the fact that this god gave them the very thing they had made possible for so many others invites an understanding of the divine and the sacred feminine that does not demand perfection or perseverance; it reveals a god who has no prerequisites for favor or blessing or love, who comes alongside us in our labor without qualification, who stays. . . .

In her story for the She Is Project, Becca De Souza writes:

> If our mothers had named the Holy One, would God
> have firstly been midwife, continually welcoming new
> life in even the most excruciating circumstances? I have
> never found God absent in my darkest nights, even when
> the pain has threatened to swallow me, even when I've
> wished that I would die because the future felt too cha-
> otic. When my heart was utterly broken, when my body
> was tangled unconscious, when I bled out my first baby
> and was separated from my firstborn after birth, even
> when I've been in the middle of a painful conflict with
> a trusted friend. God has always stayed close, putting
> pressure on my lower back, whispering truth to my incon-
> solable heart, hands covered in my blood, tears falling

with my own. She hasn't been in control of or responsible for my pain but always present, always welcoming the most possible good, the healing, the new.[7]

God as midwife. May it be so.

———— ⟪ ❦ ⟫ ————

THE MIDWIVES STORY, WHEN remembered and reimagined, beautifully invites both the reality and metaphor of midwifery, pregnancy, labor, and delivery—in birthing, in friendship, and in the most generous understanding of the divine as feminine. Admittedly, it's a thin line to walk: balancing the goodness they enable and experience with the potential pain that they and so many other women know when it comes to these very real, even visceral topics. Without neglecting or avoiding this truth, it is my deepest hope that you have encountered two women who embody that paradox, who strengthen and console, who heal and comfort, and who remind you that you are not alone, no matter what.

◇◇◇

Dear One:
When reality threatens, when "gods" demand, and when power usurps dignity, we stand alongside you in solidarity and strength. When days come in which you feel alone, barren, and afraid, we hold you close, soothe your brow, and wipe away your every tear. When you labor to bring forth all the life that grows within, we offer you every protection, support, and comfort.

We are present in every friendship you share, every pain you know, every challenge you face. We are with you in every joy and sorrow, every hope and disappointment, every birth and loss. We encourage you to cry out, remind you to breathe, and tell you to push as you bear and birth infinite beauty and wisdom. We celebrate you with endless abandon. And in all this, we stay. Always. How can we not? You are our daughter, our lineage, our kin.

◇◇◇

QUESTIONS FOR
FURTHER REFLECTION:

1. I hope you have known friendships like the Midwives had with each other. If so, what difference have they made in your life? In what ways have you been a midwife to your friends? What do you feel when you name the significance of both these realities—for you and for others?

2. The Midwives were capable of doing all that they did *because* they had each other—even and especially in places of profound fear, risk, and loss. What does this inspire or compel in/for you?

3. What do you make of the idea that the Midwives befriend *you* in the most real and present of ways? What might be different for you if you believed this?

4. The Midwives bravely disobeyed the "powers that be" and broke the rules. It was incredibly risky and potentially costly. Similarly, we are more than aware of what it will cost us to do the same. When have you taken the risk anyway? What risks might you more willingly take were you to know and trust that the Midwives endlessly remain by your side?

5. "At the very dawn of religion, God was a woman. Do you remember?" What does this summon or invite for you? Can you imagine the divine as midwife? What would that enable and invite for you?

6. Most of us struggle with the pain of loss, not having our deepest desires fulfilled, praying and hoping and pleading and bargaining and still not getting what we long for most. What can you imagine the Midwives would offer you—long to offer you? What difference might that make?

Chapter Five: JAEL

Teach your daughters their battle cries are needed far more than their silence and hear them deafen the world with their fearlessness.

—NIKITA GILL

One of the predominant reasons why scripture can be so hard to read, why it is so often—understandably—disregarded completely, is because of the violence. Book after book, chapter after chapter, generation after generation, there is violence—in families, within and between tribes, over land, and because of leadership (or lack thereof). There is violence enacted by the very god of whom these stories portend to tell: punishing sin, flooding the world, killing enemies, striking dead those who dare to disobey. And there is endless—and excruciating—violence against women.

I am never surprised or shocked by reluctance to absorb these pages, these stories, the doctrine, or the divine. Critical questions are appropriate and legitimate; we should have been asking them all along. Had we done so, all of us, all of humanity, would live in a much different world today.

With this daunting precursor, we turn our attention to the story of Jael—a violent tale if there ever was one. I often consider passing her by. But in doing so, I fear I will perpetuate a different kind of violence. When we ignore hard or confusing stories, especially those of women, we repeat what has happened all along: looking away, pretending it never happened, defaulting to out of sight, out of mind. When even one woman is unseen, unheard, and forgotten, it is that much easier to forget more of us, all of us—even for us to forget ourselves, or at least the parts of our own stories we'd prefer to just ignore.

So, I stop. I stay. I look closer.

The story of Jael *is* violent, but not in the way you might expect. It shocks. And it invites a way of being we've not considered for ourselves. I can barely imagine a world in which she serves as model and template, where she is aspiration and inspiration both. But I want to. So, I *do*. I imagine a world with Jael as mentor, muse, and the bravest of guides.

Her Text
—paraphrased from Judges, chapters 4 and 5

There was a time in which a woman named Deborah led the people of Israel. Both a prophet and a judge, she sat on a hillside under a palm tree and people came to her to settle disputes, receive her counsel, and hear her wisdom.

One day she sent for Barak, the commander of the Israelite army, and said, "Take ten thousand men and lead them up to Mount Tabor. Sisera, the leader of our opponent's army, along with all his chariots and troops, will be defeated."

Barak replied, "I will only go if you go with me."

Deborah agreed: "I will go into battle with you, but because of this, the honor will not be yours; Sisera will be delivered into the hands of a woman."

The day of the battle came. As Deborah rode alongside Barak, she proclaimed, "Now go! This is the day the Lord has given Sisera into your hands." They rode down the mountain, ten thousand men following them, and pursued chariots and soldiers until all of Sisera's troops were killed—not a man was left.

When Sisera realized that his defeat was imminent, he escaped on foot. Jael, the wife of Heber the Kenite, went out to meet him, saying, "Come in, my lord. Don't be afraid." Once inside, he told her he was thirsty. She opened a skin of milk, gave him a drink, and covered him with a blanket.

"Stand in the doorway of the tent," Sisera told her. "If someone comes by and asks you if anyone is in here, say no."

When Sisera was sound asleep, Jael picked up a tent peg and hammer and drove the peg straight through his temple into the ground.

Barak came by in pursuit of Sisera. Jael went out to meet him and said, "I will show you the man you are looking for." Barak entered the tent and found Sisera dead.

Deborah and Barak gathered all the people and sang a song to celebrate their victory. The refrain, "Blessed be Jael by women," honored the woman who brought them victory, the woman of whom Deborah had foretold.

The story of both Deborah and Jael ends with these words: "Then the land had peace for forty years."

———— ❦ ————

CAN YOU IMAGINE JAEL IN A DISNEY movie? A book assigned in high school English? A binge-worthy series on Netflix? A true-crime podcast? What if her story didn't shock us? What if, as we heard of her, we nodded knowingly? What if we doodled tent pegs in the margins of our journal? What if we aspired to her invincibility? What if we knew her as a goddess who stands with us in fierce protection? What if we had her name tattooed on our ankle? What if our inherited and embedded understanding of what it means to be a woman was courageous, brave, dangerous (in the very best of ways), and fierce?

What if, indeed.

———————— ❖ ————————

I SOMETIMES ASK MYSELF IF I COULD DO what she did; if I have it in me to do what must be done when called upon. I take some respite in the fact that her particular story is *far* from the reality of my day-to-day life. Then I realize that this is the very point: the beauty and relevance of Jael's story is that it takes place smack in the midst of *her* day-to-day life. In an unexpected but no-less-present moment, she acted in alignment with what she knew was right, she was brave beyond belief, and she astounded others (and us) with her courage.

Jael went out to meet Sisera knowing exactly who he was—a military leader bent on destruction and backed into a corner. She invited him into her tent, alone. She gave him milk and blankets. She encouraged him to sleep. And she swiftly and without hesitation struck him dead. No tallying of pros and cons. No cost-benefit analysis. No holding back. In the midst of her day-to-day life (though admittedly, a battle being fought around her), she rose up. She acted!

I think of the many houses and the women within them who hung quilts as a signpost to the Underground Railroad, promising safe passage for slaves from south to north. I think of Malala Yousafzai, the fourteen-year-old girl shot by the Taliban because she advocated for girls' education. I think of mothers and fathers trying to cross the border into the United States, legitimately fearful of having their children torn from their arms, given US immigration policy. These are not stories-of-old but of normal people, women like Jael, who made the decision, in the moment, to rise up and to act.

Would I do the same? I've had the opportunity to make bold choices in my day-to-day life *and* in the moment. But too many times, I've let caution and fear overrule what was right and necessary.

When, for example, my dad said he didn't think I should continue dating my Black boyfriend: too many obstacles, "think of the children," etc. My life to that point had been shaped by my parents' extensive efforts to expose me to a larger world, to decry bigotry of any kind, and to make sure I knew that life in our small town was *not* what life looked like—nor *should*. I couldn't believe what I was hearing. I didn't understand. But still—unwilling to refute my father's opinions and unable to bear his disfavor—I drove to my boyfriend's apartment and broke up with him that same day.

More times than I care to remember, my husband passively critiqued what I was wearing, wishing I'd chosen something more to his liking than my own. Each time, I went back to the closet and changed, never naming how it made me feel and unwilling to deal with the fallout of my dissent.

I once had a meeting with a female CEO who blatantly and angrily articulated that she had no sympathy for younger women coming up through the ranks. "I never got any support; no one did me any favors. But I made it. They can do the same." I was offended by her blatant, even ignorant demonstration of internalized patriarchy. But I only mumbled something unintelligible, not willing to rock the boat.

I read Ijeoma Oluo's book *So You Want to Talk About Race* in the midst of the nation's heated discussion (and shocking behavior) regarding white supremacy, police brutality, and so much more. I was so afraid I'd say something wrong that I didn't say much at all. My fear was stronger than my ethics or my heart, even as I read Oluo's words:

> . . . you have to try to adjust to the feelings of shame and pain that come from being confronted with your own racism. You have to get over the fear of facing the worst in yourself. You should instead fear unexamined racism. Fear the thought that right now, you could be contributing to the oppression of others and you don't know it. But do not fear those who bring that oppression to light. Do not fear the opportunity to do better.[1]

I look back on each of these scenes—and many more besides—with overwhelming regret, wishing I had, indeed, done better. My quick and automatic response, even now, is to shove them right back under the rug where I've kept them hidden—out of sight, almost forgotten. I don't like these memories, the places and times in which I was the antithesis of Jael and so many other women who have risked so much, done what was right, when it was required.

This is why I tell Jael's story, and why I wish it had been told all along: *because* of our discomfort with it, because of my own. She serves as a bold reminder of what we are capable of, not in the *absence* of fear and risk but in the midst of it. She reminds us that we have the tools at hand (as well as the ones within) to do what needs to be done—not someday, but right now and in the moment. And none of this alone: we are closely companioned by Jael, inspired by her story, infused with her courage, and strengthened by her heart.

———————— ❦ ————————

THERE ARE NOT MANY TEXTS IN SCRIPTURE that blatantly honor women. Which is what makes these two back-to-back chapters so phenomenal: the first tells of Deborah's leadership and Jael's courage; the second is Deborah's song *about* Jael. We can surmise, with relative accuracy, that had it not been for Deborah's voice, we would have one more tale of a military victory at the hands of men. And we can *know*, with certainty, that these two women—together—are who enabled this story to both happen at all *and* be told.

Tikva Frymer-Kensky, a female rabbi and feminist theologian, speaks to a lyric in Deborah's song, "Blessed by Jael by women." She says it is a call for all women to claim Jael as their heroine and even role model—that Deborah's words are a proclamation that "all women have this capacity for ferocity and courage."[2] When other women advocate on our behalf, speak what is most true about us, and call us into places of visibility and voice, we step into the honor we deserve, the strength that is truly ours, the confidence that often lies dormant. *This* is the beauty, uniqueness, and gift of women's relationships with one another.

Jael's story, in synchrony with Deborah's, calls us to look for, even expect, powerful advocacy by women. They see and call forth our strength and bravery. They compel us to dare greatly on behalf of something larger than ourselves. And they invite us to do the same, to take every opportunity to champion the advocacy that will compel another "Jael," another woman, to make her most risky and amazing choices, to stay in the fight, to rise up in unexpected, powerful, and life-changing ways. This *is* the power of women— the power that is available and infinite when we honor, trust, and love one another. This is what Jael offers us; she is both recipient and benefactor.

———————— ❦ ————————

TIMING IS EVERYTHING. JAEL WAITS. She serves. She protects. Only when trust is established and Sisera sleeps, *then* she drives the tent peg through his temple. But her story is not only about this—the murder, the weapon, the violence, the victory. She *knew* when the time was right. All doubt and ambivalence fell away. She trusted herself. There was no holding back. And when she did take action, "ferocity and courage" were hers.

As we wonder about and work within the dilemmas, questions, and decisions that are ours—even and especially when we struggle to trust ourselves—we can trust Jael. We can ask for and receive her wisdom and perspective. And we can know, with resolute confidence, that when we feel the least ferocious, least courageous, even least hopeful, Jael offers *us* warm milk, warm blankets, and rest. But she will not harm us in our sleep; she is sustaining us for battle—the ones we have yet to fight and the ones we have been fighting all along.

Between the lines of Jael's shocking and violent tale, we are reminded that we *do* know what to do and when, and that there are songs yet to be sung about us—*our* courage, *our* ferocity, and *our* endless capacity to fight for what matters. In and through it all, we can *know* and trust that Jael is by our side, that she stays. Perfect timing.

———— ❦ ————

EVEN IF WE HADN'T FORGOTTEN OR skipped right over Jael's story throughout time, the temptation has been strong to make it a bit more palatable (*adjective*: acceptable or agreeable to the mind or feelings; *synonyms*: attractive, enjoyable, pleasant, tempting, delightful, savory, sugar-coated, tasty, yummy). There is a myriad of problems with this, but foremost among them is that nothing about her actions can be accurately defined in this way or aligned with these words. To learn of her and from her, *un*palatable, even *un*comfortable, is required. And this may be her greatest gift.

We live in a world that asserts our "right" to be comfortable—and then, directly on the heels of that assertion, does everything in its power to make sure we never get too content. If we did, we'd stop buying, purchasing, and endlessly striving for more. We'd stop believing that we're *not* enough—or too much. We'd stop allowing capitalism, white supremacy, and patriarchy to dictate pretty much every damn thing. We'd fight against beauty advice, aging rhetoric, less pay, the lack of reproductive rights, stereotypes, definitions of success. We'd disallow corporate greed, the cost of and limited access to healthcare, biased news, global warming, politicizing everything under the sun. We'd reject culture's every attempt to lull us into a life that *is* palatable (and attractive, enjoyable, pleasant, tempting, delightful, savory, sugar-coated, tasty, and yummy)—as defined *exclusively* on its terms.

Jael reminds us that palatable is not the goal, not even the desire. It is *dis*comfort and *dis*content that changes anything—and everything. "Discontent is the nagging of the imagination. Discontent is evidence that your imagination has not given up on you. It is still pressing, swelling, trying to get your attention by whispering: 'Not this.' "[3] Discomfort and discontent are powerful forms of discernment. They enable us to acknowledge and admit our endless and conditioned resistance to any kind of pain. They reveal our proclivity to avoidance and create opportunities to follow the less-traveled path, the braver path, the riskier path. Radical and countercultural choices are what invite our courage, make possible our growth, strengthen our eye for injustice, and teach us that no amount of settling (or making things palatable) is acceptable. Discomfort and discontent draw Jael continually closer to our side.

I am not suggesting that we choose "hard," for the sake of it, or that we make rash and risky decisions just because. I *am* advocating, though, that we trust our inherent capacity to do difficult and scary things, that we let *our* wisdom lead us instead of what cultural or conventional "wisdom" incessantly drones on about. I am hoping that we let go of our tightfisted grip, even demand for a happily-ever-after—written into almost every story we've ever heard in order to keep us dependent, docile, waiting, and reliant. I am longing that we remember and take strength from the brave women who have gone before us, the shoulders upon which we stand. I am praying that we will kiss ourselves awake, rise up, cut through every bramble, make our own magic, and maybe even wield a tent peg to banish all that threatens who we truly are: far from palatable and Jael's daughters, her lineage, her kin.

———— ❦ ————

JAEL'S STORY ENDS WITH THESE WORDS: "Then the land had peace for forty years." It was not the battle or the war that brought about peace but one woman's courage, determination, and swift action.

I wish I'd learned this lesson far earlier. I have been too avoidant of conflict and more willing to bear the brunt of my bad decisions than deal with the consequences of potentially brave ones. To stand up for what's right can be costly. But ultimately, it is what *finally* offers us the peace we desire and deserve.

Shortly after my divorce, I was hired to lead a women's retreat at a big church. There would be close to a thousand women in attendance, and it was a perfect opportunity for me to retell some of the ancient, sacred stories I love and invite those in attendance to step into a far stronger sense of their own power, courage, beauty, and strength. Everything was in place, booked, ready to go. One tiny little detail remained: the board (all men) needed to give final approval.

I heard later that the conversation around the table that night was contentious, that more than half of them had gone to my website ahead of time and had "significant concerns." The few who were *slightly* less concerned managed to hold sway, however, and the compromise reached was that I would be "allowed to speak"— as long as I signed a statement of faith that declared my agreement with their doctrines and tenets.

When the email arrived with said statement attached, I clicked on it, scanned it briefly, and then printed it out. I neatly stacked and aligned the pages on my desk, stapled the upper-left-hand corner, poured myself a glass of wine, and took a chair at my kitchen table. I read the document once, twice, a third time—and then just sat there, stunned, confused, and in tears.

I can't sign it, can I? I did not agree with these things—not anymore. Yes, I understood them. I knew exactly what the words meant. But to put my name on the bottom of that third page would be a compromise. I would be complying. I would be giving in, somehow.

I guess I could sign it, right? And then basically do what I want. Take their money and still influence "their women." How would they ever know? The men themselves wouldn't be in attendance, that was for sure! And it wasn't like I was going to say anything radical or heretical. *Well, maybe a little . . .*

If it were today, I would not even bother printing that thing out—a waste of paper and toner. I would quickly and simply hit reply, then type two letters: N-O. Truth be told, if it were today, they wouldn't invite me in the first place.

But that was then, not now. And then, I was hurt and afraid. Every bit of what was happening felt profoundly personal. I was sucked into a vortex of doubt about my value, my worth, and certainly my words. The reaction of these men was the manifestation of *every fear* I'd ever conjured about using my voice: *Of course this is what happens when I speak up!* But underneath my hurt and fear was anger—and it didn't take long to surface. I was furious that any restraints were in place to begin with, that men sat around a table and discussed whether or not I was worthy of speaking, that the woman who had invited me couldn't or wouldn't advocate on my behalf (no women were allowed in the room for that meeting), that "permission" was required at all.

Now, with years of perspective, I can see that this was far less about the church, the doctrine, or even the men (though sadly, all of those realities remain), and far more about what was required of me. There *are* risks when I use my voice—but, far more important, there are also risks when I stay silent and follow the path of least resistance. And if there are risks either way, I'd far prefer to follow Jael's lead: choose resistance, choose myself, and boldly act.

I wish I could tell you that from that moment forward, I never again sat at my kitchen table (or lay sleepless in my bed at night) deliberating over what to do. Despite the years that have passed, neither the choices nor the costs in making them have lessened. And that still makes me angry (and hurt and afraid). But what I can tell you is that the more times I have summoned Jael's presence and acted in courageous and decisive ways, the fewer battles and wars I've had to wage. I can also tell you that I did *not* sign that statement, did *not* speak at that retreat, and never heard from the woman who'd invited me again. But I *did* have peace . . . maybe not for forty years, but certainly in the moment that I decided not to sign and most days since.

———————— ‹⊶⊙⊷› ————————

IF THIS IS THE FIRST TIME you've heard of Jael—or thought of her with more depth, intention, and compassion—I hope it's not the last. I hope you have seen yourself in her, whether in moments from your own past when you've let your determination and sense of justice override your fear or moments you yet hope for and deserve in your future. I hope you remember not only her own courageous act but also those of so many other women, known and unknown, who have had the wherewithal and strength to do what was needed, what was required, what was demanded. I hope you recognize and revel in the legacy that is yours and the fierce lineage from which you descend. I hope you hear the faint echo of the song Deborah sang over Jael, that Jael sings over you, and that is yours to sing over others. And I hope you feel less alone in your battles and fights, in difficult circumstances and impossible situations, in rest and action, and in every moment that beckons you to rise up and do what only you can do—swiftly, boldly, defiantly, and with unmistakable and unforgettable impact.

May it be so.

Dear One:

No matter the circumstances in your life—the battles that rage within and without, the fears that threaten to overwhelm, the risks and costs and consequences and compromises that endlessly persist—I am here . . . with you and for you. Remember me, call on me, and rely on me. No matter what. No matter where. No matter when. Trust me when I tell you that there will never be a time in which I won't rise up, brandish a tent peg, and act decisively on your behalf.

If you listen close, you will hear me singing—of your bravery, of your beauty, of your courage, of your strength, and of your truest identity: my daughter, my lineage, my kin.

QUESTIONS FOR
FURTHER REFLECTION:

1. Can you imagine what it would be like if your inherited understanding of what it means to be a woman in this world was modeled after Jael: courageous, brave, dangerous (in the very best of ways), and fierce? What would be different?

2. Too many times, when faced with bold choices in our day-to-day lives, we let caution and fear overrule what is right and necessary. What stories come to mind in which this has been true? How might Jael's story offer you a different narrative to follow?

3. Jael reminds us of what we're capable of—not when everything is easy and calm, but in the midst of fear and risk. When have you known exactly what needed to happen, right in the moment? What did you do? What might you do, even now, knowing and trusting Jael's presence and wisdom on your behalf?

4. Jael's story, combined with Deborah's, invites us to look for and even expect powerful advocacy by women. Where has this been true for you—where have other women called forth your strength and bravery, compelled you to dare greatly? Where have you invited this in other women?

5. Jael reminds us that "palatable" is not the goal or the desire. It is *dis*comfort and *dis*content that changes anything—and everything. What is your response to this idea?

6. There are risks when we rise up, when we choose ourselves, when we use our voice. And there are risks when we stay silent and follow the path of least resistance. What stories are yours in which you've made one choice or the other? What might you do were you to follow Jael's lead, choose resistance and yourself, and boldly act?

Chapter Six: VASHTI

*For far too long we have said yes when we wanted to say
no.... When we don't listen to our intuition, we abandon
our souls . . . because we are afraid if we don't, others will
abandon us.*

—TERRY TEMPEST WILLIAMS

I have long been fascinated by stories of royalty. In college, while
resisting my business major, I took a brief journey through
every Russian history course offered (all three of them). I was
compelled by the princesses and tsarinas, their reigns and their
tragedies. Years later, along with millions around the world, I
fell in love with and then grieved the death of Princess Diana. In
recent times, all of this has been rekindled through the fairytale-
like stories of Kate Middleton and Meghan Markle, as well as
countless films. With some reluctance, I will admit my *years*
of commitment to "princesses" like Cinderella, Snow White,
Sleeping Beauty, and Belle. Tied to my then-young daughters,
it included trips to Disneyland and the endless lure of toys and
clothes in nearly every major store.

When I look below the surface, I can (reluctantly) admit that
there's something about the fantasy, the dream, and the ideal that
still captivate me. I am aware that capitalism "capitalizes" on this
in every possible way—but there's more to it. The archetype itself
has appeal; it speaks to a core desire within. Is it the opulence,

the wealth, the power, the adulation? Being chosen, special, and set apart? Or, as the predominant Disney motif offers, is it the promise of true love and happily ever after? In Nikki Giovanni's poem "Ego Tripping (there may be a reason why)," she articulates even more of our fascination and desired truth: "I am so perfect so divine so ethereal so surreal | I cannot be comprehended | . . . except by my permission."[1] I'm quite certain it is a combination of all these: the promise, the possibility, the potential, and something dreamlike made real.

Rather than reject any of this, I'd suggest we haven't gone far enough. Underneath all that glitters is something far *more* significant and far *more* powerful. We are drawn toward these tales because deep within, they remind us of who we *truly* are: not a dress-up princess lost in pretend but a queen—noble, impossible to deny, and magnificent. Not waiting to be rescued but rescuing herself. Not hoping to be seen as worthy but never considering any other possibility. *This* is the story we really need. And it's the one we deserve to live.

To whom can we turn? Who inspires and affirms our birthright of sovereignty? Where is the queen who upends the once-upon-a-time we've known and even wished for and compels an honoring of self that far surpasses what any crown could ever provide?

Meet Queen Vashti.

Her Text
—paraphrased from Esther, chapter 1

Xerxes, the king of Persia, threw a huge party for all the nobles, military officers, and princes in his provinces. To make sure that no one could possibly ignore his wealth, power, or splendor, he had the courtyard decorated in the most lavish of ways. Gold and silver couches sat on a mosaic pavement of crystals, marble, mother-of-pearl, and other costly stones. An abundance of royal wine was served in gold goblets with ornate designs. And no limits were placed on the drinking; the king instructed all his palace officials to serve each man as much as he wanted.

The celebration lasted 180 days, and at its end he held a banquet for an additional seven days in the courtyard of the palace garden. Everyone in the fortress—from the greatest to the least—was included.

On the seventh day, when the king was in the best of spirits, he told the seven eunuchs who attended him to bring Queen Vashti into his presence, wearing her royal crown, so that all the men could gaze on her beauty.

She refused.

King Xerxes was furious. He immediately consulted with his advisors: "What must be done to Queen Vashti? What penalty does the law provide for a queen who refuses to obey her king's orders?"

One of the advisors answered him, "Queen Vashti has wronged not only you, my King, but also every noble and citizen throughout your empire. Women everywhere will begin to despise their husbands when they learn that she has refused to appear before you. Before this day is out, wives throughout Persia and Media will hear of this and start treating their husbands the same way. There will be no end to their contempt and anger. So, if it please the King, we suggest that you issue a written decree, a law that cannot be revoked, that forever banishes Queen Vashti from the presence of your Highness. Further, we recommend that the King choose another queen—one more worthy. When this decree is published throughout your vast empire, husbands everywhere, whatever their rank, will receive proper respect from their wives!"

The king took this advice and promptly sent letters to each province in his empire, proclaiming that every man should be the ruler of his own home, saying whatever he pleased.

Vashti was banished.

I *LOVE THIS STORY.* NO, NOT HER banishment; certainly not the demand that she parade herself before a sea of drunk men. I love that Queen Vashti refused to compromise herself. I love that she said no. I love (and laugh) at the way in which the king's council was rightly convinced that all women in the kingdom would be influenced by her and begin saying no themselves. I love that she held fast to *her* understanding of dignity, value, and worth—which had nothing to do with her role, her title, or her beauty. More than all else, I love that when we reimagine and retell her story, we find ourselves companioned by a queen, by *this* queen, as we remember that we are one as well.

I love that *you* are companioned by a queen, by *this* queen, as you remember that *you* are one as well. Vashti reminds you that you have a council of your own that is ever at your beck and call: your intuition, your knowing, that deep and reliable voice within. She reminds you that you can and must trust yourself, your "yes" and your "no," no matter what. She reminds you that how you see yourself matters far more than others' approval. She reminds you that who you are, truly and without question, cannot be taken from you; you are royalty, through and through. She reminds you that when it seems like all is lost, you will do well to always choose what matters most: your very self. She reminds you that you do not walk alone, ever. You are her daughter, her lineage, her kin.

So, let her take your hand as you ascend your throne and don your crown. Let her stand regally by your side as you rule, as you reign, as you live and love. Let her draw near when much is demanded of you. Let her give freely of her experience, her wisdom, and her comfort. Let her laughter, her overflowing joy, her endless encouragement and praise, and her everlasting pride *in you* heal your heart and strengthen your soul as you follow in her footsteps, fully embodying all of who you are: noble, impossible to deny, and magnificent.

Did I mention? You are companioned by a queen, by *this* queen, as you remember that *you* are one as well.

I GET IT: IT'S DAMN NEAR IMPOSSIBLE TO think of ourselves as queens. Especially amid day-in and day-out squabbles and struggles, inner voices that never sleep, to-dos that never end, and a world that seems intent on reminding us that we are not and never will be *all that*. But part of the reason we struggle to see ourselves as sovereign is because of the romanticized image we hold of what a queen's life must be like. Everything is easy and carefree; servants respond to her every whim as she moves from decadence to decadence, event to event, gown to gown. But when that is the image we hold, we avoid acknowledging the responsibility she carries—the weight of decisions that impact an entire population, how constant the sacrifice of her own desire for the collective need. Winston Churchill once said of Queen Elizabeth, "Well do we realize the burdens imposed by sacred duty upon the Sovereign and her family."

We witness the same in the story of Queen Vashti. Hardly the stuff of fantasy, in many ways it is far closer to tragedy and exactly the opposite of what we idealize and want—for her and for ourselves. There is no happily-ever-after, no rescuing fairy godmother, no prince/ss riding in on a white horse. She exemplifies her version of "sacred duty" as a nonnegotiable devotion to her own value and worth. And she calls us to do the same. When we understand our own sovereignty through her lens, we are compelled to acknowledge our stature, our dignity, and our worth in a world that desperately seeks to undermine them all. We stand tall, speak boldly, and step forward with strength while simultaneously acknowledging just how much doing so may cost us.

Queen Vashti invites us to an upside-down-and-backwards realm where losing everything is how we gain, where letting go of control is how we hold on to it, where saying no is what enables the yes that always matters most. *This* archetype, *this* way of being, is regal and responsible, extravagant and humbling, empowered and compassionate. Oh, the goodness, wisdom, and reign that is ours when we are accompanied by Vashti's story, her example, her presence, and her heart.

———— ❦ ————

THERE WAS A RADIO-THEN-TV SHOW that ran from 1940 to 1964 called *Queen for a Day*. It opened with the host asking an audience of mostly women, "Would YOU like to be Queen for a day?" Contestants were introduced and interviewed, one at a time, as they told of a recent financial or emotional hard time they'd been through. The host would then ask each woman what she needed most and why she wanted to win the title. According to Wikipedia, their requests were often for medical care on behalf of a chronically ill child, sometimes a new washing machine or refrigerator.[2] An applause meter was then used to select the winner—the harsher the situation and the more sympathy garnered, the higher the audience applause would go. The chosen woman was draped in a sable-trimmed, red velvet robe, given a glittering crown, placed on a throne, and handed a dozen long-stemmed roses to hold while her list of prizes was announced: the help she'd requested, plus extras donated by advertisers. Finally, the host would sign off with his trademark statement, "This is Jack Bailey, wishing we could make every woman a queen for every single day!"

The show—one of the earliest precursors to reality TV—made millions of dollars for the network and was later dubbed by its longtime producer, Howard Blake, as the worst program on television. In her book *What Women Watched: Daytime Television in the 1950s*, author Marsha Cassidy writes, "*Queen for a Day* explicitly tied the reconstitution of distressed women to material goods and beauty."[3]

Sadly, *very* little has changed. Material goods and beauty are what "reconstitute" us still, what promise to restore us, what we're told will enable us to feel like a queen ... or at least a better version of ourselves. Female lifestyle empowerment brands inundate us with image after image, post after post, and ad after ad of products and programs that are guaranteed to make our appearance, our homes, our jobs, and our very lives just as perfect as the women who make the promises.

The women at the helm of these . . . enterprises market to women with images of their professionally beautiful selves and their enviable lives. They do it in the guise of building a relationship with you, but what they're doing is dramatizing the gap between your ordinary apartment and their New York loft, their frequent and fabulous holidays and your staycations, their flat abs and your squishy stomach, their nearly-naked yoga and your see-through yoga pants (the ones that their inventor never intended for your kind of ass, after all), their famous besties and your toxic friends, their bottomless bank accounts and your overdraft. This kind of . . . lifestyle marketing relies on you internalizing the comparison between their exteriors and your interior, feeling bad about your present and fearful about your future, and then buying an individual solution for your individual problem from them. Because obviously they've got it all figured out. . . . They explicitly market themselves as role models and leaders-of-women but balk at assuming the risks and burdens of substantive cultural leadership.[4]

We're promised all the benefits of being a queen without the honest acknowledgment that every bit of it is illusion, false promise, and *not at all* worth aspiring toward. Until we look clearly and closely at Queen Vashti.

She stands before us as the epitome of "assuming the risks and burdens of substantive cultural leadership." She adamantly refuses any promise of ease or "honoring" of her beauty as a bargaining chip. No game show host, applause meter, king, or female lifestyle empowerment brand can confer or deny her worth. Instead, shoulders back, head held high, and with the slightest smile, she speaks a resounding no. She is a glorious manifestation of sovereignty that needs no reinforcement via someone else's approval, wants, or whims. She cannot be bought for any price.

I wish I could say the same.

Sometimes, instead of sleeping, I scroll through Instagram late into the night. I can *almost* imagine all that is promised on that small screen when I compare it to the day I've just had—far from anything remotely resembling a castle or a crown. I flit past seemingly perfect lives of glamor and ease, wealth and self-worth, beauty and esteem. My fingers hover over words that promise me relief, respite, and dreams come true, as though my personal fairy godmother will appear the instant I swipe right on "purchase," or "learn more," or "buy now." I *so* want to feel like I am enough. I have wanted it for as long as I can remember. . . .

When I was a girl, I was convinced that I was ugly and unacceptable. I know this is unreasonably harsh, but it accurately describes what I internalized and believed. My earliest memory of this "truth" emerging occurred in elementary school when a boy on the playground told me my knees were fat, laughed, and then ran to his friends. In middle school I envied my prettier friends who magically understood how to attract the opposite sex—which was, clearly, the only thing that really mattered. By high school, I was crying myself to sleep way too many nights—especially when I wasn't asked to homecoming, the Winter Ball, or prom. During my senior year, I remember standing in line for class pictures and getting yet another unedited opinion from one of the boys in my grade: "You'd actually look pretty good if it weren't for your face." Throughout my twenties, frustrated at being single, I was convinced that if only I were prettier, thinner, and more desirable, *then* I'd be chosen and loved. In the fifteen years of my marriage, my husband consistently praised my appearance, but too often in ways that felt objectifying—a means to an end. When I started dating again in my late forties, I fell in love with a man who would occasionally ask me if I was "chunking up," then tell me he was only kidding. (We're no longer together.) And do not get me started on the world of online dating: what attracts, what generates likes or messages, what solicits any hope whatsoever for anything remotely resembling a mature and mutual possibility.

As I recount even these few stories, I am aware that I carry and embody so many more—whether I remember them or not. I know they are perpetuated, over and over again, by the world in which I live. I feel the lump in my throat and the heat that rises to my face. I nod through tear-blurred vision as I read Ani DiFranco's words:

> For a girl, the fear of not being pretty is the fear of not being a valuable object, which is the fear of not being loved. It is a conflation that is instilled so early on and runs so deep that, even when you know it's a fear perpetuated by patriarchy, goaded by fashion magazines, and used to manipulate you into buying stuff, you still can't stop the way it affects you.[5]

. . . you still can't stop the way it affects you.

But some nights, instead of being unable to stop the way it affects me—endlessly reinforced via Instagram—I remember Queen Vashti. She gently calls me back to what is true and has always been true: my worth and beauty are not up for debate, display, or applause meters of any kind. I fall asleep and dream of a world in which women are seen, heard, valued, and honored for who we are—not what we look like or what we are too often pushed to contort ourselves into. And when I am awake, truly awake, I know that Vashti's story, when reimagined and retold, is what heals and transforms my own. Still. Ongoing. Always.

A GOOD FRIEND RECENTLY TOLD ME about finding just the right book on puberty for her ten-year-old daughter. She ordered the one most highly recommended, and when it arrived, thumbed through to get a sense of the content. At about the halfway point, she suddenly pulled a pair of scissors from a drawer and began cutting out pages. As her daughter watched in shock, she said, "This whole section on body size and shape has got to go! It's the patriarchy *already* telling you what's acceptable and how to become some ideal that has been determined to be most preferred and valued. I don't want you listening to *any* messaging about your body, *anyone* telling you what you should and shouldn't eat, *anyone* expressing an opinion about how you look. No!"

I tell this story because it is astonishing and rare. I tell it because I wish it were mine—on my own behalf and as a mother of daughters who never considered taking scissors to *the very same book*. I tell it because unless you are very, very lucky, you did not grow up experiencing anything remotely close to this. I tell it as a direct counterpoint to the far more common story that you, me, and nearly every woman throughout time has heard: Your worth is commensurate with your beauty. You do *not* meet the standard. You are *not* acceptable as you are. You must try harder, change, morph, and aspire to what the collective "we" (i.e., patriarchy) deems desirable. You are not enough. (And you're way too much.) I tell this story because what my friend told her daughter is, at core, what we desperately need to hear and believe: "You are worthy. Do not listen to the lies."

"There comes a time when you have to decide whether to change yourself to fit the story or change the story itself," writes Laurie Penny in her book *Unspeakable Things*. "The decision gets a little easier if you understand that refusing to shape your life and personality to the contours of an unjust world is the best way to start creating a new one."[6] Queen Vashti invites, if not commands, that we change the story itself—refuse to believe anything less than what is and always has been true: You are more than enough and *never* too much. She summons forth an end to the lies, the demands, and the judgment. And she stands alongside us even now, scissors in hand, as she cries out, "No!"

A FEW YEARS BACK, I PARTICIPATED IN an extensive leadership assessment that was compiled from responses by my bosses, my peers, and my direct reports. When all the results were in, I was given a comprehensive evaluation of my strengths and weaknesses, both self- and other-defined. As you might expect, my eyes went straight to the negative. Two words were all I could see: compromise and compliance. Interestingly, this feedback came exclusively from the team I supervised. And within the attached comments I could hear their plea: "You are better than this, Ronna. We see the pressures being exerted on you from above. Stand tall. Don't give in. We know what you are capable of."

I could have taken this as generous encouragement—the kindest of invitations to what they had witnessed in me, just how much they believed in me. Instead, I was furious. Not with them, but with myself. Somehow, bit by bit, I had chosen to not make waves, to sustain the status quo, to not push back . . . even though everything in me disagreed with the directions we were taking and the decisions that were being made. Underneath all my rationalizations, I was afraid: afraid that if I spoke my mind, exerted my opinion, and actually led, that I'd be ostracized—or, worse, terminated.

I could hardly believe that I'd let it come to this. This was *exactly* what had happened in my marriage. This was *exactly* what I'd worked so incredibly hard to change and heal: to *not* compromise, to *not* comply, to *not* sacrifice myself on the altar of others' expectations, needs, or demands. How was it possible that I was in *exactly* the same place yet again? A "no" rose up in me—one that was probably out of proportion to the situation but fueled by too many memories of when I'd been incapable of it. I made the choice, right then and there, to speak my mind no matter what, to boldly exert my opinion, and, yes, to truly lead.

Within a matter of months, I no longer worked there.

One moral to this story is that my fears were justified, that my compromise and compliance were about legitimate self-preservation. But at least in this instance, I chose a different moral: I was not willing to be afraid of being myself. Just like leaving my marriage, this decision was hardly without cost. But I could clearly see that the cost would be even greater if I stayed. (You should know that there have been *far* more times in which I wouldn't have been able to make this decision—when in fact I did not. I wasn't ready and could not bear the risk, whether financially or emotionally.)

It's almost always complicated, saying no. Our compromises seem insignificant; we barely notice them until the bit-by-bit becomes impossible to ignore (sometimes by others before ourselves). And too often, we compromise as a learned, even understandable choice—putting others ahead of ourselves. It seems preferable to risking relationship, belonging, intimacy, income, safety, familiarity, even love. The possibility of losing any of them feels as though it far outweighs the potential costs of our compliance.

Which is why Vashti's story matters. We desperately need to be reminded of what sovereignty looks like, what strength can cost, and what our dignity is worth. Without her in mind and heart, we are at the whim of a world that repeatedly asks us to show up in ways that please "a drunken crowd." The voices within get louder and louder, telling us that we are not enough, so we compromise and comply all the more. We forget from whom we descend.

Vashti's final decree was her boldest and most powerful. Had she bowed to the king's command, she would have diluted her role, her title, her very dignity. She saw that within one singular compromise lay a host of others: she would perpetuate a system of dominance and power that she clearly did not agree with, she would ostensibly tell all the women within her purview that they should concede as well, and she herself would ultimately be less royal, less herself, and far less whole. Though one could argue that her "yes" might have secured her status, her comfort, her future, her leadership, the possibility of greater impact, and even her legacy, just the opposite was true. All because of her "no."

That "no" reverberated through the land and compelled hasty policy decisions. It cost Vashti the throne. It gave rise to her erasure and, for all we know, the loss of every benefit, every privilege, every kindness. It moved her from fame to anonymity—from a sense of belonging to one of isolation. And it revealed how profoundly she understood her truest value and worth.

Even more powerful than the example Vashti sets is the compassion she offers. In intimately understanding the complexity of our "no," she can, better than most anyone else, acknowledge just how hard it is *and* extend us the kindest of invitations at the same time: "Stand tall. Don't give in. I know what you are capable of. You are my daughter, my lineage, my kin."

A SMALL BUT HARDLY INCONSEQUENTIAL detail of Vashti's story is often lost in its telling. While King Xerxes was hosting all the men, she was hosting all the women who had traveled with them. Disallowed from the men's festivities, they depended upon the queen's hospitality. And she did not disappoint. In some traditions it is said that Vashti provided a banquet for those women—drinks and sweets chosen especially for them, rooms ornately decorated on their behalf. But beyond the luxury and pampering, here is what matters most: when Vashti said no to her husband, to the king himself, she did not do so in isolation. She was in full view of many, many women—the wives, consorts, mistresses, and slaves of men with power. And I am convinced that her awareness of this compelled her courage even more.

But for all that she knew of her impact, she could not possibly have anticipated that I would be writing of her today, that you would be reading of her today, that we would be inspired still, all these centuries later. This *is* what results when any woman takes a stand on her own behalf and, whether fully aware of it or not, on behalf of the women around her, both now and into perpetuity.

Your impact is just as profound and just as lasting as Queen Vashti's when you refuse to compromise yourself, when you leave a job or a marriage, when you walk away from the church, when you outwardly express your inner strength and determination, when you trust your clear sense of right and wrong, when you claim your own sovereignty.

Not quite convinced? Think of the stories you've read and their protagonists, the women from whom you've taken inspiration, think of all the ways in which you have been strengthened and sustained in a particular moment or given much-needed encouragement to carry on by those women. Jane Eyre. Anne Frank. Mary Frances Nolan in *A Tree Grows in Brooklyn*. Meg Murray in *A Wrinkle in Time*. Helen Keller. Amelia Earhart. Rosa

Parks. Julia Child. bell hooks. Maya Angelou. Oprah Winfrey. Ketanji Brown Jackson.

One response would be to look at this list and instantly feel that you don't compare. But I beg to differ, as does Vashti herself. Your bravery can't help but engender courage in others. Your love for your children, your friends, your world can't help but change the future. Your opinion in a meeting at work can't help but redirect the trajectory of any number of realities—and lives. Your journal writing, your blog posts, your someday memoir, your screenplay, your emails, and your texts can't help but expand our minds, our perspectives, our hearts. Your "no" *and* your "yes" can't help but tilt the earth on its axis. You make that much of a difference.

This is no small or inconsequential detail. Let it be a not-so-secret knowing you carry within. A certainty you hold close. A confidence that compels you every single day. The belief that you are, indeed, a queen . . . a living, breathing honoring of the women in whom you have taken inspiration.

Know this, as well: Queen Vashti bows in *your honor* when you see yourself as she does—a woman of undeniable distinction, impact, power, beauty, and courage. Today, tomorrow, always. And all of this *just* by being you.

As I am writing about Vashti, news has filtered in about documents leaked from the Supreme Court that tell of the possible overturn of *Roe v. Wade*. Were this to happen, it would eliminate a woman's choice to say either yes or no. It would erase our voice, our will, our agency . . . our sovereignty. How is this possible? I feel like I've somehow been evicted from my home, displaced, wandering the streets and uncertain about where I belong. It's as though everything I thought I knew, everything I trusted as true, has been taken from me. What once seemed relatively stable and certain is turned upside down and shattered into a million little pieces.

And then I realize this is hardly a metaphor. Vashti knew all of this *literally*: dethroned and cast out, everything taken from her, turned upside down, and shattered. My trauma is not new to her nor the thousands of women before and since. My awareness of this hardly makes it better; in many ways, it makes it worse. But when I can acknowledge this—the history that persists, the misogyny that demands its own way, the endless machinations of men to get what they want and throw a fit when they do not—I am reminded, yet again, that I am not alone. I am reminded, in the words of Nadia Bolz-Weber, that "sometimes the most holy thing we can say is: No. Not on my watch."[7] I am reminded that I am part of a long and beautiful line of women who continue to fight and to hold fast to our rights, our ownership over our own bodies, our irrevocable identity and worth, our right (and demand) to say no.

I would like to believe that had Vashti's story been told differently from the get-go (and Eve's, Cain's Wife's, Hagar's, the Midwives, and countless others') the reversal of *Roe v. Wade* would not even be a consideration right now. I would like to believe that we would instead have a history filled with story after story of a woman's resolute "no." I would like to believe that no councils or decrees, kings or husbands could keep us constrained, compliant, or silenced. I would like to believe that hearing Vashti's story anew today might be enough to revive and restore us, to remind us of the lineage that is ours, to encourage us to take our place alongside all the women who have fought and fought and fought some more, who have not given up, who have continuously held a vision of what this world can yet be.

I would like to believe all of this. I *do* believe all of this. It's just particularly difficult today.

Dear One:
I know you feel the dull ache of compromise—the temptation to say yes when what you want to say is no. And I know just how much it costs. Just how risky it is. How swift and severe the consequences. Oh, how I wish it were otherwise. But for all my wishing, I know this with complete and immovable certainty: you deserve a life that honors who you truly are—a queen in your own right, capable of bearing every privilege and every responsibility with dignity, courage, and grace.

So, on days when your choices are the hardest, trust my presence and strength within. Hear me when I say that you cannot be bought or swayed. No matter what anyone else says, demands, or tries to take from you, straighten the crown on your head and remember that you are beautiful, worthy, and sovereign. Speak your truth with shoulders back and head held high. And trust that when it is heard, when you are heard, whole worlds will change—including your own. This is your legacy, your bloodline, your inheritance, your impact, and your throne to claim, for you are my daughter, my lineage, my kin.

QUESTIONS FOR
FURTHER REFLECTION:

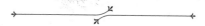

1. When you think of royalty—of a queen, even a princess— what first comes to mind? How have those thoughts been influenced by stories, media, even capitalism? How does Vashti's experience as a queen shift or shape what it means to be sovereign?

2. In what ways has social media influenced either/both your desire to feel like you *are* enough and the sense that you are *not* enough?

3. Let's go back to Ani DiFranco's words: "For a girl, the fear of not being pretty is the fear of not being a valuable object, which is the fear of not being loved. It is a conflation that is instilled so early on and runs so deep that, even when you know it's a fear perpetuated by patriarchy, goaded by fashion magazines, and used to manipulate you into buying stuff, you still can't stop the way it affects you." What is your response to this? How *does* it affect you?

4. Think about the stories in your own life where "no" was too costly to speak. What difference might it have made if you knew of and could trust the presence of Vashti alongside you in that moment?

5. Think about the stories in your own life where you *did* have the courage to say no. What did it cost you? How did those experiences strengthen or support your sense of self, your value, your worth? What do you imagine Vashti wants you to know of what she witnesses in you?

6. Can you see the ways in which your choices, you *just* being you, influences and impacts the women around you . . . now

and in the future? When you consider such, what resistance shows up? What does it invite?

7. What would be different, even on a day-to-day basis, if you truly believed that you *are* Queen Vashti's daughter, her lineage, her kin?

Chapter Seven: ESTHER

Courage doesn't always roar. Sometimes courage is the quiet voice at the end of the day saying, "I will try again tomorrow."

—MARY ANNE RADMACHER

In *Women Who Run with the Wolves,* Clarissa Pinkola Estés tells of a dream she once had:

> . . . I was telling stories and felt someone patting my foot in encouragement. I looked down and saw that I was standing on the shoulders of an old woman who was steadying my ankles and smiling up at me.
>
> I said to her, "No, no, come stand on *my* shoulders for you are old and I am young."
>
> "No, no," she insisted, "this is the way it is supposed to be."
>
> I saw that she stood on the shoulders of a woman far older than she, who stood on the shoulders of a woman even older, who stood on the shoulders of a woman in robes, who stood on the shoulder of another soul, who stood on the shoulders . . .[1]

Despite the years I've spent reimagining and rewriting these stories—even though I know them by heart and have, time and again, experienced their presence and wisdom and power—I still forget that I am part of their lineage. I still forget that so many women have gone before me—that they pat my foot even now, steady my ankles, and smile up at me. I still forget that I do not live my story in isolation, adrift and disconnected, but instead surrounded, supported, even uplifted. And I still forget that others already and will yet stand on *my* shoulders.

I forget until I remember Esther. . . .

Queen Vashti's "no" is what enabled Esther's "yes." Their stories and lives were inextricably linked. In Esther's darkest moments, she must have taken great encouragement and strength from the amazing woman who preceded her—the shoulders on which she gratefully stood. Vashti must have known the same somehow, aware of who followed in her footsteps. She would have heard the stories of Esther and realized that in some mysterious and sacred way, her courage was what emboldened this young girl to do such incredible things. And for sure, she must have smiled.

Her Text
—paraphrased from Esther, chapters 2–9

Once the king's wrath had cooled, he couldn't help thinking about what Queen Vashti had done and what had been decreed against her. His attendants tried to lift his mood by suggesting that he appoint emissaries to gather up every beautiful young virgin into his harem. "You can choose the one who pleases you most and she will reign in place of Vashti," said one. This suggestion pleased King Xerxes and the plan went into place.

A man named Mordecai, a devout Jew exiled from Jerusalem, lived in one of the royal precincts. His cousin Esther—more like his daughter, as he had cared for her since her parents died—lived with him. When she was captured and taken to the palace, he was distraught. He made her promise that she would not reveal her nationality or any information about her family, believing this might keep her safe. And every day he walked back and forth in front of the entry to the harem, hoping to hear what had become of her.

Twelve months passed. During that time, every woman held captive was taken through an elaborate beauty treatment intended to make them as desirable as possible to the king, and every night, one of them was called before him and then returned to the harem the next morning. Of them all, the king chose Esther for his queen and placed the royal crown on her head. Then he threw a great feast in her honor for all his officials and servants, granted a holiday to the provinces, and bestowed generous gifts.

Even then, Mordecai returned to the gates and listened for news. One day he overheard two guards plotting to assassinate the king, and he sent a message to Esther in time for her to warn him. The conspirators were hung on a gallows and Mordecai's brave actions were recorded in the official history of the kingdom.

Not long after, the king granted special honors to a man named Haman, one of the most prominent princes of the realm. All the people bowed down to him when he was in their presence—except for Mordecai, who adamantly refused. This enraged Haman, so he hatched a plan to annihilate every Jew in the empire. He informed the king of their sedition, paid 10,000 silver talents to write the decree of their punishment himself, and even conspired with his wife and advisors, all of them casting lots to determine the date for this heinous event.

The edict was written, sealed with the king's signet, then distributed among the people. Mordecai was distraught when he heard the news. He informed Esther of Haman's plot and said, "You must go to the king and beg for your people to be spared." Esther reminded him of the law: no one was allowed before the king unsummoned; unless he held out his golden scepter to her, she would surely be killed. Mordecai responded, "Do not think that you will escape genocide because you are in the king's house, any more than all the other Jews. If you remain silent at this time, relief and deliverance for the Jews will arise from another place, but you and your father's family will perish. Who knows if perhaps you were made queen for just such a time as this."

Esther summoned all of her resolve and told Mordecai, "Gather all the Jews together and fast for three days and nights. My maidens and I will do the same. Then I will go to the king. If I perish, I perish." At the end of her fast, Esther dressed in royal apparel and bravely went before the king. He was pleased when he saw her and held out his scepter, saying, "What do you request of me, Queen Esther? I will give it to you—up to half my kingdom!" Esther humbly asked that he and Haman come to a banquet that very night. It was her intention to expose Haman and his plot, catching him unawares. But when the opportunity came, fear got the better of her, and she could not go through with it. Instead, she asked if they would join her for dinner again the next night.

That evening, Haman saw Mordecai sitting at the king's gate and became so incensed over his refusal to bow down that he ordered gallows constructed immediately. He had every intention of getting the king's consent the next day to see Mordecai hung on it.

That same night, when the king couldn't sleep, he asked one of his attendants to read some of the official histories to him and was reminded of Mordecai—the man who had saved his life. When he asked what honor had been given to him, he was dismayed to discover that nothing had ever been done. Determined to remedy the situation, the king called for whoever was in the court. Haman responded first as he was there early to get the king's permission to hang Mordecai. But before he could speak, the king said, "What should be done for a man the king desires to honor?" Convinced the king was speaking of him, Haman replied that he should be dressed in a royal robe and led on one of the king's horses through the city streets with this proclamation: "This is a man in whom the king delights!" The king said, "Go at once! Get the robe and the horse and do just as you have suggested for Mordecai the Jew! Do not neglect anything you have recommended." Haman begrudgingly did as he was commanded and then rushed home in grief, telling his wife and his advisors everything. At the news she said, "You will surely come to ruin!"

For the second night in a row, Haman and the king attended Esther's banquet. This time she bravely spoke, explaining the situation and pleading, "If I have found favor with you, Your Majesty, grant me my life and spare my people." Outraged, the king asked, "Who is he? Where is he—the man who has dared to do such a thing?" Esther replied, "It is Haman!" The king stood up in a rage, left his wine, and went out into the palace garden. Haman, realizing his fate was in Esther's hands, stayed behind to beg for his life. But when the king returned and saw Haman falling on the couch where Esther was reclining, he exclaimed, "Will he even molest the queen while she is with me in the house?" The king's guards seized Haman and hung him on the same gallows that had been constructed for Mordecai.

Esther went before the king a third time unsummoned. He held out his scepter yet again and listened as she pleaded with him to reverse Haman's decree—an edict that would annihilate her people. The king explained that he could not revoke any document sealed with his own signet, but he would issue notice to the entire kingdom and inform them of every detail. This allowed the Jews to not only be prepared but to be victorious in battle. In memory of their deliverance, the Jewish people established an annual feast called Purim that is still celebrated today—as is Esther and her courage on their behalf.

UNLIKE SO MANY OF THE STORIES I reimagine, Esther does not need my help. No other woman's story in this sacred text has been told, replicated, and enacted as frequently as hers. Understandably! There is a king, a villain, a harem, and a beautiful young woman who is orphaned, captured, favored, and crowned queen. The dramatic plot takes unexpected twists and turns. It's the stuff of the best fiction, let alone historical narrative.

At least sixteen films were produced between 1910 and 2013 that told some version of Esther's story[2]; a musical was also made in 2018, and countless TV documentaries and dramas exist. When it comes to books—whether biography, theology, or fiction—the list is long. And if this weren't enough, Esther is one of only two books in both the Hebrew and Christian scriptures that are named for a woman and do *not* mention God.[3]

Shockingly, these distinctions have not spared her from controversy, argument, even gender bias. Commentators, scholars, and theologians over time have actually argued that the Book of Esther should give men every mention of honor and that she should be shamed:

> The book's indifference to religious practices, its dubious sexual ethics, and its female heroine continued to baffle commentators, particularly male Protestant commentators. . . . The tendency among scholars was to exalt Mordecai as the true hero of the tale and to downplay or even vilify the role of Esther. . . . [Her] sexual ethics in particular are called into question. "Esther, for the chance of winning wealth and power, takes her place in the herd of maidens who became concubines of the king."[4]

This is *not* the predominant interpretation of her story, but still . . .

It is mind-boggling.

How can anyone possibly make the leap from a woman being sex-trafficked and imprisoned in a harem to *using* sex on her own behalf; from risking her life for her people to being seen as a small-and-barely-necessary pawn in a man's game; from being placed in horrific situations with tremendous risk to a narrative that assumes her every motive is power and privilege?

Mind-boggling and infuriating.

Despite Esther's popularity, her story *as told* has reinforced patriarchal stereotypes: beauty is a woman's primary asset, she uses it to get what she wants, and it is the predominant tool she wields to manipulate men—even if for the best of reasons.

Mind-boggling, infuriating, and very familiar.

A college student reports a rape but is told she didn't say no clearly enough so must have wanted it. A wife claims domestic violence but is not taken seriously because she doesn't press charges. A mother longs to protect her children from their father's abuse but cannot afford to leave him and is shamed for staying. A female employee names sexual harassment but is fired instead of promoted. Another female employee *is* promoted but then accused of sleeping her way to the top. A woman finds out she is pregnant and chooses abortion but knows that any say over her own body has been taken from her.

It is easy for me to get up on my soapbox and rant, easy for me to scream and rage and demand that women—past, present, and future—be treated with the dignity deserved, have our voices heard, our stories believed, our choices honored, our courage celebrated, and every possibility of our harm eradicated. What is hard is living in a world that continues to perpetuate just the opposite. What is hard is figuring out how to walk through a single day—let alone a life—in which our value, worth, and choices remain up for debate. What is hard is trying to discern when to fight, how to feel about ourselves when we don't, and what to do about the fact that too much of the time it doesn't seem to make any difference.

It is against this backdrop that Esther's story *must* be reimagined and remembered. When we fail to do this, we lose sight of a woman's truth: we (still) face and bear extremely painful circumstances, we (still) make excruciatingly difficult and risky choices, and we (still) summon undeniable courage. We *must* hold fast to who Esther was and all that she did despite her youth, her fear, and the potential consequences. And we *must* stand firm in who *we* truly are: royalty—wise, brave, and deserving of every honor.

ESTHER MUST HAVE WISHED QUEEN VASHTI'S story had gone a completely different way. *If only Vashti had not been so beautiful. If only the king had not asked her to appear before him. If only she'd said yes instead of no.*

We are like her in this regard.

When we find ourselves in the hardest of circumstances and the most painful of stories, we inventory all of the plot lines, decision-points, and people that led to this exact moment in time. We hear ourselves say, "If only . . ." repeatedly. If only our mother had left our father sooner. If only our friend hadn't moved away. If only our boss had advocated for us instead of looking the other way. If only our sister hadn't gotten in the car that day. If only that breakup had never happened. If only we'd stood up for ourselves. If only we'd said no instead of yes.

But there comes a time—sometimes invited, other times inevitable—in which we can no longer dispute the path that is ours or the truth of our reality, no matter how much we may dislike or fear what lies ahead. There comes a time in which we must acknowledge that we *do*, in fact, have agency and choice. There comes a time in which we know, without shadow of doubt, what is required of us. There comes a time in which we can *and do* claim the story and life that is, after all, our own. And when that time comes, *every time* that time comes, there is no one better than Esther from whom to learn and upon whom to depend.

———— ❦ ————

WHAT WAS IT LIKE FOR ESTHER TO go from being a young girl who lived in the safety and familiarity of her cousin's care to becoming queen? She could hardly have been ready to wear the crown, to be waited on hand and foot, to understand either the privilege or the cost of what was now hers by decree and right, for all that would yet be required. She woke up one morning, looked in the mirror, and had to reconcile herself to a new and powerful identity.

We tend to think of stepping more fully into our sovereignty and who we know ourselves to be as something incremental, part of a larger arc and journey. We get stronger bit by bit. We demonstrate courage one step at a time. But Esther's story holds a far bolder invitation and more urgent timeline. She calls us to take on the powerful identity of a queen right now. No delay. This morning. This mirror. This you.

What if we accepted her invitation? What if, like her, we woke up, looked in the mirror, and recognized the title and role that is just as much ours as hers? What if we didn't wait for it to be bestowed upon us but instead deemed ourselves ready, worthy, and fully sovereign even now? What if we walked through our days wearing a long and dramatic velvet robe and the most beautiful of crowns—if only in mind and heart? What if no one else needed to see it for it to be real and true? What if we made decisions and choices with an unshakeable awareness of both our privilege and our responsibility? What if we remembered that it's not the castle, the servants, the wardrobe, or the jewels but the resolute belief in who we truly are that makes us royal?

I'll admit that this has been hard for me to imagine, let alone swallow, on the many days when I've woken up to dishes in the sink, sick kids, and money worries. One morning, shortly after my husband and I had separated, I opened the front door only to discover that my car had been stolen overnight. Hardly a queen's carriage, it was a 1980-something Honda that no one in their right mind would bother taking—or so I thought.

Nothing regal or royal stared back at me from the mirror that day—most days, really. And it is on *exactly* these days and in *exactly* these circumstances that I hear Esther's heart on my behalf: "Wake up, Ronna. See yourself as I do: regal, royal, crowned a queen. Not someday, when things are perfect, but right now. *Nothing*—not dirty dishes and or sick kids or money worries or stolen cars—can change this reality, this truth, this you: a woman of distinction and title, power, and worth. Remember who you are. Remember who you are. Remember who you are. No delay. This morning. This mirror. This you."

I desperately want this shift in identity and self-perception to happen overnight—for you, for me, for all of us. I know it seems impossible, but in many ways, its far-fetchedness heightens my desire: I want all women to wake up one morning, this morning, knowing exactly who we are and what is ours to do. Saying what must be said, even when it's hard. Changing everything. Reigning in brave and beautiful ways. And stepping into our respective worlds, velvet robes and crowns intact, impossible to sway from what we resolutely know and believe: we are Esther's daughter, her lineage, her kin.

—————— ⟨⟩ ——————

THERE HAVE BEEN MANY BRAVE WOMEN throughout time whose courage we've honored and admired. What we don't know enough of, though, is their fear. Often wielded as inspiration, their stories prove, even demand, that we can and must be fear*less*, too. Refrigerator magnets and overly repeated phrases abound: "Never let your fear decide your fate." "Be fearless in the pursuit of what sets your soul on fire." "Life begins where fear ends." "With God, I am fearless."

I'm not *against* courage. I simply prefer that we tell the truth about our fear—its presence, weight, even texture and smell—instead of locking it behind a facade of confidence and bravado or, worse, denying it altogether.

This is yet another reason why I love the story of Esther—why it matters, why we deserve to know of her, take inspiration from her, and find solace in her courage . . . and her fear.

It is true: the text itself leans toward her courage, but we can rightly assume fear's intimate proximity. When ripped from the only family she knew and sex-trafficked straight into the king's harem. When, after twelve months of forced preparation, she was presented to the king for his use and pleasure. When she was chosen as his queen. When Mordecai told her that she *must* go before the king and expose Haman's plot. When she hosted the first dinner party and was so afraid that she could not go through with her plan. When she did finally speak up and expose Haman's vicious plan. When the king left her chambers to go walk in the garden and she was left alone with the very man she had accused. When Haman was killed, but the decree to eradicate her people remained in place. When she stood before the king—unbidden for a third time—to ask that he undo his own edict. When he told her he could not. When the day of battle came. Over and over again, her life reflects both fear *and* courage, with no attempt to banish one and glamorize the other; instead of all or nothing, coexistence.

With this as our example, we can take heart when our lives look and feel the same. Our fear and courage coexist when we choose to speak up in our own home—especially when it disrupts the status quo. Our fear and courage coexist when we have to decide whether or not it's worth it to tell our boss what we really think, or to report sexual harassment to human resources, or to ask for a raise—let alone time off, more maternity leave, or a flexible work schedule. Our fear and courage coexist when we walk across an open parking lot in the dark. And, as I've named multiple times, our fear and courage coexist when we reckon with the messaging from media, family, and even within that tells us we are "not enough" and "too much."

We need and deserve the reminder and reimagining of Esther's story as we live our own. We need and deserve to be companioned and encouraged by someone who knows the angst and ache of being caught between fear and what must be done. We need and deserve her presence alongside us when we stand, when we speak, and especially when we do not. We need and deserve to know that she stays, constantly reminding us that we are not alone, no matter what. In our courage *and* in our fear.

———————— ⊰⊱ ————————

MY FAVORITE MOVIE OF ALL TIME IS *Strictly Ballroom.* It tells of Scott, a competitive ballroom dancer who wants to perform his own steps instead of following the strict rules within ballroom tradition. He faces the ostracization of friends, deals with his mother's blatant chagrin, loses his partner just weeks before a significant competition, and even concedes at one point that he cannot win if he follows his heart. Fran, the female lead, exists in little more than the background for the first third of the film—sweeping the floors of the studio, taking beginner dance classes, being arm-twisted into buying makeup the mother sells on the side, getting berated and almost completely ignored. At one point she confronts Scott, acknowledges his non-regulation steps, and asks to be his partner. He laughs at her and then says she has no right to approach a champion with such a foolish and ridiculous idea. She boldly and tearfully responds, "*Vivir con miedo es vivir a media!*"

A life lived in fear is a life half-lived.

There's more to the story, of course—scene after scene in which fear drives almost everyone's incessant demand that Scott comply and conform (along with fabulous costumes, a great soundtrack, the best humor, and some incredible dancing).

The first time I watched this movie was late on a Friday night. I had been in a theology class of some sort all day and was bone tired. But I was also determined: I *would* make it through the film, even though tomorrow's alarm would come in the form of my then-toddler girls waking up *far* earlier than I might hope. Staying up, as it turned out, was not a problem; in fact, the moment I saw the red curtains close over "The End," I got up from the couch, poured myself another glass of wine, restarted the DVD, and watched it all over again from start to finish. Since then, I've probably seen it at least another twenty times. I still get choked up when Fran nearly shouts the phrase above. I feel the tears behind my eyes when Scott's father admits that both he and Scott's mother have "lived our lives in fear." I smile and cry at the same time when Fran's courage does not eradicate her fear but compels her to risk anyway and enables the same in Scott. And I sit a little bit further forward on the edge of my seat when the two of them dramatically take to the ballroom floor to perform a dance that is unlike anything anyone has ever seen ... or allowed.

It somehow doesn't matter that I know exactly what will happen in every scene and can quote almost every line by heart. For me it is always a beautiful and poignant reminder of just how much courage it takes to live in a world that demands our conformity, insists we stay in line, and shames us for anything else. I am repeatedly inspired by the way it reveals courage *and* fear in partnered step—two halves of a life wholly lived. And sometimes it reminds me of Esther (another story I know scene-by-scene and line-by-line)—a woman who *both* tentatively and bravely danced her own steps and generously invites us to take her hand and follow her lead.

HAD ESTHER BEEN TOLD WHAT she would one day accomplish, she would have said it was far more than she could do, beyond what anyone could expect of her, and completely impossible. She could not have seen the huge and sweeping plot that was developing around her. She could not have acknowledged the bigger narrative of which her seemingly small life was a part. She could not have begun to understand how significant her life and story truly were. Esther could only live her life one moment at a time.

She risked, but not always. She spoke up, but not always. She stepped forward, but not always. She took in distressing news, faced (often horrific) circumstances, and acted as best she knew how and could. And when all was said and done—over years of time (not days or even moments, as the story often sounds)—she became a queen, a legend, a woman worth every honor and praise.

The same is true about you.

The minor and seemingly *in*significant moments of your life are often what make the biggest difference. Paying the bills, having yet another conversation with your kids, telling your spouse or partner the truth, avoiding Amazon.com as a salve for your broken heart, sitting down to write the book that only you can, choosing to vote, expressing your honest opinions. Saying yes and, to be sure, saying no. Risking, but not always. Speaking up, but not always. Stepping forward, but not always. Taking in distressing news, facing the hardest of circumstances, and acting/being as best as you know how and can.

These are the moments, hardly insignificant, in which Esther offers you all her compassion, solidarity, and strength. These are the moments in which you can hear her whisper the words that Mordecai spoke when *she* was most afraid: "Who knows if perhaps you were made queen for just such a time as this." These are the moments that make all the difference and, when all is said and done, make you and your life legendary. You just don't know it yet.

ONE OF THE HARDEST ASPECTS OF Esther's story and, quite frankly, almost every story within this sacred text, is the harsh and violating use of power over women. It makes us hesitant, if not resistant, to read the stories at all. There is so much harm, so much exertion of dominance, and a shockingly endless justification of all of it by religious communities and their leadership. So when, as women, we do the hard and necessary work of questioning and critiquing the wielding of power in our own lives and even those of others, it can be incredibly difficult to return to (or hear for the first time) stories that perpetuate it. It can feel irrelevant, damaging, and perhaps even irresponsible to continue telling them.

I once received an email from a woman who asserted exactly this: "Don't you feel that retelling these women's stories from scripture just reinforces, even repeats, the harm they have known? Wouldn't it be better to stop telling them, as they have done nothing on women's behalf? Instead, they have made things worse." I can see her point, and there are definitely days when I'd like to follow her logic. But on far more days, I continue to tell them *because* of her point: these women deserve to be known in ways that blatantly declare their harm and decry it instead of silencing it. They deserve to be remembered and honored as shining examples *for us* of what it looks like not only to endure but also to convert power in new, healed, and beautiful ways.

Esther offers and reveals what power can look like and all that it makes possible when accepted, stepped into, and utilized with compassion and care. But admittedly, most of the time, this feels more like an anomaly than a possibility. Our history is fraught with countless women who have been burned at the stake, raked over the coals, shamed and silenced for the slightest expression of personal power. We are inundated by far too many examples of power *still* exerted in the most entitled and irresponsible of ways:

war, police brutality, environmental disregard, gun control, legislation that places decisions about a woman's body in hands other than her own. We know that power *is* ours to claim—personally and collectively—and also that our past and present experience of it is little other than devastating. It's no wonder we cringe and feel profoundly conflicted at the same time.

It is Vashti, Esther's predecessor, who demonstrates the power we prefer: an unwavering belief in her value and worth no matter the pressure to conform or the costs of refusing such. She makes a political choice when she boldly rejects male expectations and demands. She influences the women in her proximity through her adamant refusal to bend to the patriarch's will. Her form of courage is required in these days of the #MeToo movement and so much more. Her story models power through direct confrontation, with a blatant declarative of "no."

And yet Esther's story feels far more familiar. She demonstrates power in ways we find harder to accept and, quite frankly, often work to reject. We don't want to stay a moment longer in oppressive relationships, jobs, or situations—and yet Esther does. We are frustrated by and tired of having to work within "the system"—and yet Esther does. We are determined to no longer accede to compromise, let alone compliance—and yet Esther does. She tolerates and endures more than we would ever wish for ourselves or any woman—and all on behalf of something far larger, even systemic. She reveals quiet, even stealth-like, actions that women often employ—because we must. Her story models power that is subtle, with a tentative declarative of "yes":

> Esther was in the same situation that many women are in . . . they do what they need to do in order to survive. And sometimes, through subversion, cleverness, or simply taking advantage of unexpected opportunities to exercise influence, they can go beyond survival and bring about change.[5]

Esther is hardly alone. Irena Gut was a Nazi officer's house-keeper who hid twelve Jews in the basement. When he discovered them sometime later, she agreed to become his mistress in exchange for his silence and every one of them was saved. Harriet Tubman made some thirteen missions to rescue close to seventy enslaved people through the Underground Railroad—a network of antislavery activists and safe houses. It wasn't until much later that her brave efforts were known, her power celebrated. The Midwives, discussed earlier, disobeyed the Pharaoh and not only demonstrated their own clandestine power but also honored the power of every woman who brought life screaming into the world while under threat of a son's death. Tamar disguised herself as a sex worker and became pregnant with her father-in-law's child to claim the protection and promise that had been withheld from her. Abigail circumvented her husband's idiocy and pride by over-stepping the boundaries of a woman's expected role to save her people from a king's wrath. Rahab hid enemy spies on her roof in exchange for the protection of her family. The Wise Woman of Tekoa disguised herself in order to provoke King David to recon-ciliation instead of war. Jael invited an enemy commander into her tent, offered him warm milk and a blanket, then killed him while he slept. I could go on. And Esther, of course, is a distinguished part of this lineage of power as well.

I wish that Esther could have accomplished all she did with-out the harm—that the Jewish people could have been saved in any way other than through her personal sacrifice. I wish the same for Irena Gut, Harriet Tubman, and every woman listed above—along with so many more. I wish that all women, then and now, could do far more than just survive. I wish that no kind of "subversion" was ever required to exert and express our power. I wish that all of us, like Vashti, could declare our "no" when any situation, context, relationship, or person dares to compromise our integrity, our sense of self, our worthiness. I wish we could *always* stand tall and defiant, refusing to be held back, mistreated, unseen, silenced, disrespected, or disregarded in any way—and all without consequence.

But in the meantime, in the day-in and day-out reality of our challenges (and our compromises), I am deeply grateful for Esther's story, wisdom, and power-full presence. She reminds us to trust that what we yet endure *is* on behalf of something larger that we cannot foresee. She calls us to believe that we are never without power—whether demonstrated in the most bold or tentative of ways, and inclusive of tremendous risk. She compels us to boldly tell our own stories of "no," "yes," and everything in between. She longs for us to reimagine and retell *her* story so that we are reminded we are not alone in ours.

Dear One:

I lived in a world where those with absolute power determined my fate, where every choice seemed taken from me, where any sense of my dignity and worth was bruised then buried as I was groomed to please the king. I wish I could tell you that being chosen and crowned offered me respite, courage, and strength. In many ways, it demanded even more of me.

Your story need not be like mine (and I pray it is not). But when decisions press, demands overwhelm, darkness reigns, hope feels lost, your courage falters, and saying yes feels more like the end of all things than a beginning, take heart. Every step of my own perilous journey has brought me to you. Right now. No delay. For such a time as this—and always.

I remain with you, for you. I hand you your royal robe and glittering crown—both of which you have earned and deserve. I see every glimmer of your dignity and pride. And I endlessly remind you that your brave and beautiful choices will change everything. That you do change everything, every day.

It is my deepest honor to call you my daughter, my lineage, my kin.

QUESTIONS FOR
FURTHER REFLECTION:

1. Esther stands on the shoulders of Vashti, and you stand on the shoulders of them both. Who else can you count in the legacy of endless support that is yours? What does it feel like to acknowledge that you are accompanied, even held up, by so many women from throughout time?

2. When does "if only" get the better of you? How might Esther's willingness to step forward anyway offer you encouragement and strength?

3. Esther had no time to somehow become a queen. One day she was a young girl. The next she wore a crown. She calls us to do the same—to take on the powerful identity of a queen right now. No delay. This morning. This mirror. This you. What comes up for you when you consider *just* doing this? What makes it hard? What might be different if you could achieve it?

4. What grace might you experience if you allowed courage and fear to coexist? What if you didn't have to banish one in order to demonstrate the other? What if you imagined Esther alongside you in both?

5. Esther's version of power is not as desirable as Vashti's. She is ambivalent. She is afraid. She is inconsistent. And unlike Vashti, she stays in a situation that requires immense compromise—all on behalf of an entire nation of people. Which form of power feels more familiar to you? How do you discern when one is called for vs. the other?

6. What is the "for such a time as this" that is distinctly yours? How might you imagine and believe in Esther's presence alongside you in exactly this? (You can, you know.)

Chapter Eight:
THE CANAANITE WOMAN

Nevertheless, she persisted.
—Spoken by Senator MITCH MCCONNELL
about Senator Elizabeth Warren, February 7, 2017

Hers is not the easiest or happiest of stories to tell. In addition, it's admittedly confusing. But because it has survived and even exists at all, because this woman's voice has been sustained over time, I cannot help but believe there is much that she longs for us to know and understand about her . . . and ourselves. Especially in places where we are desperate for help, where our needs feel unheard and disregarded, and—perhaps above all—where the divine seems distant and even unsympathetic to our plight.

As difficult as her story is, she offers us a profound invitation into the legitimacy of our desires, our determination, and our unquestioned deservedness.

Meet the Canaanite Woman.

HER TEXT
—paraphrased from the Gospels of Matthew, chapter 15, and Mark, chapter 7

Jesus left the village he'd been visiting and withdrew into the district of Tyre, staying in a house he hoped would keep his presence secret. But a Canaanite woman heard that he was close by, found him, and began to cry out, "Have mercy on me, Lord, Son of David; my daughter is demon-possessed and suffering terribly."

He did not answer. But his disciples begged him, saying, "Send her away because she keeps shouting at us." He responded to them, "I was sent only to the lost sheep of Israel."

Undeterred and desperate, the woman bowed before him. "Lord, help me!"

When at last he finally spoke to her directly, he said, "It is not good to take the children's bread and throw it to the dogs." Without skipping a beat, her retort landed squarely: "Yes, Lord, but even the dogs feed on the crumbs which fall from their masters' table." Jesus said, "Woman, your faith is great; what you wish shall be done for you."

She went home and found her child lying on the bed, the demon gone.

———— ⟨✥⟩ ————

THE JEWISH PEOPLE (JESUS'S OWN LINEAGE) saw themselves as exclusive, honorable, and chosen by their god; all others, especially the Canaanites, were considered a polluting presence and threat to the sanctity of Israel. Strike one.

She was a woman. Strike two.

She did not stay hidden or silent, as was customary, preferred, and nearly demanded. Instead, she hunted Jesus down and was inconsolable in her cries, her request, her demand to be heard. Completely unacceptable. Strike three.

I'm not one to use sports analogies; still, the Canaanite Woman was ostensibly eliminated from this game before it even began. But even with three strikes and a certain out, she argued with the "umpire." And instead of getting thrown out of the game—as is always the case in baseball—she ultimately got both her way and the win.

Jesus's response to her, to be sure, was shocking. *She* was shocking—in the most beautiful, bold, and insistent of ways. And this is exactly the inspiration we need, not only when things are difficult, unjust, and painful, but every single day, every single moment. She persisted; she refused to allow anything short of the answers she knew she deserved; she was immovable in her demand to be seen, heard, and honored.

I grew up with the well-worn adage of "Because I said so." This was an oft-repeated phrase when I asked, "Why?" Why I had to do something. Why I *couldn't* do something. Why I couldn't *have* something. A catch-all response from one parent or the other, it clearly meant "Don't ask me any more questions." The first time I heard myself say the same words to one of my daughters, I winced.

This and messages like it, whether out loud or nonverbal, become engrained within us—*accept what you're told, don't argue, don't push back*—especially when they come from people who are older, wiser, and/or more powerful than us. And so we comply—until we lose it, until we blow, until we can't stand it one more second. (Or until we completely shut down our every thought of agency, our every exertion of will, our every need and desire.) Whether a young girl, a teenager, or a grown woman, we are forced to straddle an invisible tripwire: docile compliance on one side and "out of control" on the other. Neither honors our inherent worth, nor does walking on the eggshells of in-between so as not to upset anyone or anything. Yet our just and appropriate questions, our challenge of the status quo, and our legitimate rage have not been allowed. Even, it seems, by ourselves:

> Even the incipient suggestion of anger—in themselves or in other women—makes some women profoundly uncomfortable. In an effort to not seem angry, we ruminate. We go out of our way to look "rational" and "calm." We minimize our anger, calling it frustration, impatience, exasperation, or irritation—words that don't convey the intrinsic social and public demand that anger does. . . . Anger is usually about saying "no" in a world where women are conditioned to say almost anything but "no."[1]

We need a model of what it looks like to stand our ground, to demand both answers *and* what we desire. And it is this, exactly, that we receive in the story of the Canaanite Woman. She says "no" to Jesus's "because I said so" response. She refuses to be cautious of the invisible tripwire. She is not the least bit committed to looking "rational" and "calm." She is not remotely concerned by others' assertions, opinions, or demands. *She* demands! She demands that Jesus answer her. She demands that he respond directly to her request. She demands respect. She demands what she came for, what she believes he has the power to grant, and what her daughter deserves. And in making those demands, it is safe to say that she also demands we do the same.

Her demand of us does not come from a place of anger *at* us, but *for* us; it's a call to our rightful agency and liberation. She longs for her story to be the only permission we need to blatantly and boldly say no to the insipid expectation that we dare not ask for more—that we do not ask, period. She reminds us that "because I told you so" will not do, whether from a parent, an authority . . . even a god. The Canaanite Woman shows us that no matter how many strikes are against us, sometimes (even often) the rules of the game do not apply: we deserve to be honored, seen, and heard. After all, we descend from a sacred lineage of women who have endured and persisted, and through whom we inherit strength, courage, and will.

THERE'S ANOTHER STORY TOLD OF JESUS in which, once again, he is traveling from town to town. Along the way, he sees a widow weeping at the death of her son and brings the boy back to life. He's not asked to do this; his heart is touched by her loss of the son who would have cared for his mother, who would have provided for her welfare, who would have carried on the family line. In yet another instance, Jesus *does* heal a daughter—but only at the insistent request of her father, an esteemed religious leader within the community.

This story, the Canaanite Woman's story, does not include a son or a father. It is about a woman—a mother—and *her* daughter.

Daughters carried little significance at the time. In the story of Hagar, Abraham and Sarah wanted a son. In the story of the Midwives, the Pharaoh was only concerned that boys be killed at birth. In genealogies within this same text, it is rare (and hugely significant) when daughters—any women, for that matter—are mentioned. The perpetuation of the male bloodline was all that was longed for, heralded, and celebrated; it was even seen as proof of divine favor.

So, we are lucky to have her: the Canaanite Woman. As stated earlier, the mere fact that her text has survived throughout time, especially given just how controversial it is, is evidence of her tenacity—but also of something far deeper. She proclaims and embodies a message that refuses to be silenced or ignored no matter how much time passes, no matter how much preference and privilege is given to boys and men (then and now), no matter how many rules are created and laws are passed (or unpassed) to keep us silenced, insignificant, and small. Daughters matter. Mothers matter. Women matter.

It is easy to get lost in other aspects of her story. I'll get to those later, but this is the very point: it is so tempting to take our eyes off her; to wonder about and even debate everything else, and in the process lose sight of her.

Sadly, this happens all the time, both accidentally and with great intent.

Eighty-five women accused Harvey Weinstein of inappropriate to criminal behavior ranging from requests for massages to intimidating sexual advances to rape.[2] We are distracted by his fame, his legal battles, his fall from grace. In effect, *we* are seduced—by design—to take our eyes off the women themselves, to not look at (or vehemently rage against) the larger, systemic, and shockingly offensive cultural realities that would allow such a thing to happen in the first place.

There is nothing definitive to prove that the Super Bowl is the largest human trafficking event in the world. But when we take our eyes off the women, we also lose sight of the fact that in 2021, 96.4 million viewers tuned in to the Tampa Bay–Kansas City matchup *and* that same day over 40 million people (the vast percentage of which were women and girls) were trapped in modern-day slavery.[3]

There are consequences when we take our eyes off the women. In her book *Invisible Women*, Caroline Criado Perez says:

> The impact can be relatively minor. Shivering in offices set to a male temperature norm, for example, or struggling to reach a top shelf set at a male height norm. Irritating, certainly. Unjust, undoubtedly. But not life-threatening. Not like crashing in a car whose safety measures don't account for women's measurements. Not like having your heart attack go undiagnosed because your symptoms are deemed "atypical." For these women, the consequences . . . can be deadly.[4]

It's hard to look closely, to stay focused and intent on so much that is hard, painful, and unjust. Especially when we know there is no end to the stories, the consequences, the reality women have faced and do still. But once again, that is the very point:

The Canaanite Woman refused to look away. And she disallowed anyone else from doing the same. Yes, she was in a marginalized, even shunned, social strata. Yes, daughters didn't matter all that much. Yes, the disciples wanted her to go away. Yes, Jesus was rude to her. But still, always, she kept her eyes fixed on what mattered. Her daughter's restoration remained her North Star.

And thankfully, *she* is *our* North Star. A lighthouse in the sea of misogyny. A sacred guide on whom we can depend no matter what we must endure and overcome. As she fights for her daughter, so too does she fight for us: her daughters, her lineage, her kin. And she gives us the motivation and courage to do the same. *We* remain focused on what matters. *Our* priorities remain clear. *We* persist. *We* argue. *We* shout what she did: that women—past, present, and future—deserve to be restored, healed, and honored. Just like the Canaanite Woman, we will *not* be denied.

May it be so.

———— ❦ ————

THE PHRASE QUOTED IN THIS chapter's epigraph, "Nevertheless, she persisted," was used in an attempt to silence Senator Elizabeth Warren during a debate over the nomination of Alabama Senator Jeff Sessions as US Attorney General. Part of her statement was a recitation of Coretta Scott King's 1986 letter in which her own opposition to Jeff Sessions' appointment as a federal judge was articulated. Senate Majority Leader Mitch McConnell said, "Senator Warren was giving a lengthy speech. She had appeared to violate the rule. She was warned. She was given an explanation. Nevertheless, she persisted." The phrase was immediately adopted in hashtags and memes to refer to any strong woman who refuses to be silenced. Perhaps the Canaanite Woman was the one who started the trend. More likely, she was one of many who preceded even her—a legacy of women who have refused to be silenced.

But just like Senator McConnell, Jesus's disciples weren't having it. They didn't want to listen. They didn't want to deal with her incessant longing or heartfelt pleas. She was too loud, too emotional, too sad, too demanding—too much, too much, too much. "Send her away because she keeps shouting at us." Not "Send her away because we don't know how to help her." Not "Please heal her daughter." No. Their ask was not about her at all; rather, it was an unwillingness to be inconvenienced or made uncomfortable in any way. "Don't make us stand face-to-face with a woman's desires and demands."

A woman who cries out, who continuously asks for what she wants, who raises her voice in order to be heard, has been called, and still is called, a nuisance and a shrew. She's "militant," "up on a soapbox," "a troublemaker." As though speaking calmly works. As though simply stating what we want, need, desire, or deserve will be heard and honored. No, it seems that we *must* cry out, endlessly, simply to be heard let alone responded to and respected.

It seems that very, very little has changed since the story of the Canaanite Woman.

And once again, I can't help but wonder how this trend might have turned far sooner if this woman's story had been told by way of example—as a model of strength, a way of being, a demonstration of what is not only required but appropriate. Once again, I have to believe it's not too late. Clarissa Pinkola Estés is right: "If you have never been called a defiant, incorrigible, impossible woman . . . have faith . . . there is yet time."[5]

We can and must keep crying out—with the *change-everything* awareness that we are never alone in doing so. We are companioned by an infinite lineage of solidarity and support: Eve, her daughter-in-law, Hagar, the Midwives, Jael, Vashti, Esther, and countless more besides. Together they repeat the truest words, those that we most need and deserve to believe: *Persist. You cannot possibly be too much. You are our daughter, our lineage, our kin.*

———— ❦ ————

IT IS A SCARY, EVEN ABSURD, THING to desire, to dare to ask for what we want, to hold on to the hope that we will be seen, heard, and answered.

I have often chosen what seemed a far safer route. I have shut my desire down completely—no crying out, no praying, no wanting. I have turned off my feelings altogether, thinking that to be the wisest and sanest choice—definitely preferable to facing disappointment and feeling my heart break yet again. Being single. Infertility. In the darkest days of my marriage. As a mother. Being single yet again . . .

I divorced more than sixteen years ago. Early on I assumed I would meet someone and remarry. But as more time (and more time still) has passed, it has become shockingly easy to *not* desire relationship at all. This is especially true when I even remotely consider the perils of online dating—of which I have had my fill. It is exhausting to peruse profiles, swipe left or right, engage in casual chit-chat that rarely goes anywhere, and weed through too many men who, at least from the safe distance of an app on my phone, do not begin to meet my expectations. "My life is complete, satisfying, and amazing without a man, without a partner!" I say to myself. This is both accurate and honest. But so is this: I need to ask myself what I *really* want, reconnect with my desire, and then, no matter what answer comes, allow myself to "be" with the ache that the question often provokes.

The ache is inevitable, I believe. And it is far more. I have come to see it as evidence of something beautiful, compelling, and oh-so-wise: evidence of my very heart. Despite the hurt I have known, the fears that have often overwhelmed, and multiple disappointments along the way, my heart has never led me astray.

Desire is this absurdity that holds open the infinity of possibility. Ever optimistic, ever resourceful, desire tells us what it sees as it speeds ahead on its divine wings. What we cannot see, desire describes, and then it goads us to travel on until we have given birth to Joy.[6]

Let me be clear: this is not to say that I will return to online dating. But at the end of the day, what I have learned (through much trial and error *and* through the profound and powerful story of the Canaanite Woman) is that desire is not what hurts. *Not* desiring is what hurts. *Not* desiring is what is scary and risky and daunting.

The only alternative or antidote I have been able to find to all of this—the ache, the risk, the disappointment, the fear—is settling for less. And if there is anything the story of the Canaanite Woman teaches, invites, and compels, it is that this is *not* to be my fate.

Or yours.

IT MUST BE ADDRESSED: JESUS'S ODD, even insulting response to this woman. Scholars, academicians, language experts, theologians, clergy, and even mere mortals have attempted many explanations—most of which fall short for me. There is tremendous pressure to make sense of something unquestionably upsetting, but instead of just letting it *be* upsetting, the attempt at justification makes things worse.

It has been said that in equating the woman with a dog, Jesus was "testing her faith" or that he was speaking with a smile on his lips. But this does not account for the fact that no such insults appear anywhere else in the Gospels, or how inappropriate either of these things would be in the face of a child's illness. Yet another argument holds that the use of the word for "household dogs" rather than "wild dogs" softens the insult, but this hardly makes a difference—"little bitch" is no improvement over "bitch."[7] Some have surmised that their back-and-forth dialogue (if you could call it such a thing) fits a common pattern in ancient literature where a subject approaches their leader with a request that is initially dismissed, then later conceded to. "In this kind of exchange, the leader is shown to be just and fair and the subject is judged virtuous. Both receive public honor . . ."[8] *Mm-hmm.*

Here's what I make of it:

First, Jesus's response, even lack thereof, undoes the incessant demand of perfection—in God's self and in my self. I am deeply encouraged by the probability that perfection was never the innate state of the divine and is therefore neither required nor expected of me. Second, I am introduced to a god to whom I can relate and who can relate to me—a god who clearly knows and understands *my* frustration, *my* impatience, *my* exhaustion, because that god knows the same. It is pure grace: a god who does not roll their eyes at my emotions or behavior, a god who does not even entertain the thought that maybe, one day, I'll finally get it together.

Third, it is a relief to know, even trust, a god who does not make sense. In fact, it's what I far prefer: a god who is nothing close to what I was taught and told, what I expected, and even what I sometimes think I want. Instead, this is a god who is impossible to define, explain, or pin down. "If I find Him with great ease," wrote Thomas Merton, "perhaps He is not my God. . . . If I find Him wherever I wish, have I found Him?"[9] Naturally, I would change these pronouns, but Merton's sentiment rings true. Even more, it is consistent with what we are given in the Canaanite Woman: every preconceived notion, deified image, and centuries-defended character of the divine goes out the window. Thank god!

To be sure, many of us have learned of and leaned on a god who is absolute, immutable, inviolable, infinite, all-knowing, in control. There is comfort to be taken in this, to be sure; but how much more reassurance and accessibility might we find in a god who is complicated—a god without boundaries or limits of any kind, self-imposed or assigned? In her book *Wholehearted Faith*, author Rachel Held Evans writes, "If the story is strong enough to be tried and tested, surely the God who is the ultimate author and inspiration of that story is strong enough—and tender enough—for our explorations too . . . I've always been bothered by the argument that our wonderings and wanderings inevitably send us sliding down that proverbial slippery slope."[10]

The Canaanite Woman's story is the opposite of a slippery slope—instead, solid ground. She draws our vision back (or perhaps ahead) to what makes all the difference and matters most: not the god but *her*—her faith, her hope, her belief. For what is the point or purpose of any of these—faith, hope, belief—if they are not alive, vibrant, and intimately held within? Their very existence, let alone fervency, is dependent upon us—not what, where, or in whom we place them. Faith, hope, and belief cannot be given. They cannot be commanded or demanded. They cannot be required. All three are developed, tried, tested, strengthened, and sustained by *our* lives, *our* struggles, *our* challenges, and *our* perseverance. We remain faithful and hopeful on behalf of that which we most desire in spite of our questions and doubts, in spite of our disappointments, and sometimes even in spite of our *dis*belief. And it is in *response* to this that the divine responds to us—not as test or prerequisite but because the divine's heart cannot help but be moved by our own.

It is this, specifically and extravagantly, that we witness in this woman's story. She pleads, she demands, she persists, and she determinedly holds fast to her faith, her hope, and her belief that her daughter must and will be healed. And after all the back-and-forth, Jesus says, "Woman, your faith is great; what you wish shall be done for you." Not "Your faith *in me* is great." No. It was *her* faith that brought forth her daughter's restoration, reclamation, and wholeness—everything the mother desired and the daughter deserved.

I know this begs an impossible-to-ignore question: what are we to do when all our faith, all our hope, and all our belief do *not* result in our desires being met? I wish I had an answer—one that would suffice, that would explain everything, that would make sense of far too many circumstances that go in the exact opposite direction of what we wish. This story is not enough solace (there can *never* be enough in such places), but when I return to it, its complicatedness offers me context, perspective, and rest. Because I cannot make sense of Jesus-as-divine in this story, I can better hold all that is complicated in my own life, in the lives of those I love, and in the world as a whole. It is this story's ambivalence th gives me the needed space to allow my own. And it is know god who relents, who *does* acknowledge and honor my fai hope, and my belief—who sees me, hears me, and even I do—that makes it at least a little bit more palatable to carry on, and keep asking, demanding, and desiring.

Though I could walk through each of Jesus's cryptic re line by line—parse them out, explore the original Gree provide exegetical insight—I don't think it matters . . . at le enough. What *does* matter is that the Canaanite Woman endures it all, pushes back, stands firm, and holds fast to what she believes he can do for her. She bravely demonstrates that *she* is who we can depend upon in this story: to show up, to fight for what is just and right, to persevere on behalf of *her* daughter . . . just as she does for us. Still and always.

No matter how impossible my reality, how improbable its resolution, how distant and distracted God seems, the Canaanite Woman stays. And she understands—in the most precious and personal of ways. No answer to prayer. No fix. But the consolation and assurance that I am not alone in any of it. Sometimes, some days, this is just enough to get me through.

———— ⟨◦⟩⟨◦⟩ ————

FOR ALL THAT FRUSTRATES ME ABOUT THIS story, and in spite of the less-than-stellar light it casts on Jesus, it provides incontrovertible evidence we would not otherwise have: the divine has a tender and fierce heart for women. How else can we explain why her story has survived? How else are we to understand why a text that is so derogatory of the man whom it purportedly honors would be included, let alone kept as is?

I often think that the fact that *any* woman's story has survived the centuries, the scrolls, the scribes, the translations, the subjectivity that abounds—is proof of the Sacred Feminine. Especially the story of the Canaanite Woman. There has to be a distinct and not-to-be-ignored power that has kept Her finger on stories like these, who has intervened when men have thought to let them go, who has consistently let Herself be seen . . . when we look, when we desire, when we believe.

TODAY WE MIGHT DIAGNOSE THE Canaanite Woman's daughter's condition as mental illness, or perhaps epilepsy. In ancient Greek, one of the meanings of the root word "demon" is "to throw apart." In other words, anything that disintegrates us, anything that divides us, anything that destroys our wholeness, is demonic.[11] But above and beyond the naming of what "possessed" the girl is one undeniable fact: the Canaanite Woman could not, would not be dissuaded from saving the person she knew her daughter to be at core. She knew the qualities and characteristics of her child like the back of her own hand. She knew the girl she loved vs. the one that was twisted into something unrecognizable. She knew her daughter's heart. And I have to believe that had her argument with Jesus not gone as it did, she would have hunted him down again and again. She would have risked anything and everything (and perhaps did) to have her daughter back, healed, and whole.

We can read a story like hers and wonder how it relates to us. Our cries haven't been answered. We do not feel deeply known; sometimes, in fact, we are unrecognizable even to ourselves. Our heart is not heard. We are not healed and whole. We want her happy ending.

What if the story of the Canaanite Woman is an invitation to believe that *she* knows us—who we are at core, our truest and best qualities and characteristics, our deepest heart? What if her story is an invitation to trust that she longs for and believes in our healing and wholeness as much as she did her own daughter's? What if her story is an invitation to allow that much desperation and determination, that much ferocity and faith, on our own behalf? What if her story is an invitation to believe that we are worth that kind of fight, that level of sacrifice, that amount of vulnerability, that much passion?

It's almost too hard to imagine that someone would advocate for us in these ways, with this much commitment and dedication—almost too hard to believe. But if we *could* imagine it, if we *could* believe it, if we *could* dare hope for such a thing, if we *could* allow and acknowledge our desire for exactly this? *Mmmmm.*

Maybe it feels too fantastical to consider such a thing. Maybe it pushes you just a bit too far outside your comfort zone to consider that this ancient, sacred woman could be that close, that intimate, that kind of mother *for you*. I understand your skepticism, believe me. But then there's this: it was also too fantastical for her to hope as she did. It was way outside her comfort zone to believe. And yet. And yet . . . every bit of what she longed for *was* what she received.

If we can allow for the miracle that was hers, perhaps we can allow for the same on our own behalf—by and from the Canaanite Woman herself. This *is* how close, how real, how present I believe her to be. This *is* exactly what I believe she generously provides. This *is* what I believe every one of these women's ancient, sacred stories offers *you*: the much-deserved miracle (and day-in, day-out lived experience) of being seen, heard, supported, and loved—far beyond what you've ever dared imagine. This *is* what you're endlessly invited to not only believe but also receive.

That *would* be a happy ending, yes?

<><><><><><><><><><><><><><><><><><><><><><><><><><><><><><><><><>

Dear One:

In your every desire and disappointment, I have raised my voice. In your every hope and grief, I have kept shouting. When you have longed for healing—your own, others', and that of your world—I have persisted, fought, and stayed. And when you have wanted nothing more than to be heard, to be seen, to be acknowledged, I have longed to take you in my arms, to wipe away your tears, to hold you close, to remind you that you are worthy, you are not too much, you are loved.

Now, will you believe that this is so? Will you let your faith return? Will you take my hand—healed and whole—and walk into every challenge that awaits, every sickness that threatens, every argument that is yours to win, knowing that you do none of this alone? It is all I've ever wanted for you. And it is what I will continue to give to you, always. You ARE my heart—my daughter, my lineage, my kin.

<><><><><><><><><><><><><><><><><><><><><><><><><><><><><><><><><>

QUESTIONS FOR
FURTHER REFLECTION:

1. How familiar does "because I said so" sound? How acquainted are you with the deeper messages of *accept what you're told, don't argue, don't push back*—especially with people who are older, wiser, and/or more powerful than you? What does the story of the Canaanite Woman invite in light of this?

2. How might the Canaanite Woman's persistence invite you to the same on your own behalf? What do you long to fight for with that much determination? What if you weren't alone in doing so?

3. I have named just how scary it is to desire, to ask for what we want, to hold on to the hope that we will be seen, heard, and answered . . . especially by the divine. What do you make of the way in which the Canaanite Woman responds to all of this? In what ways might she encourage you to desire anyway?

4. How do you respond and react to Jesus's way of being with this woman? How might this contradict what you have come to learn and believe about the divine? Are there aspects of *this* god that offer you encouragement? What might those be?

5. When you consider the aspects of your story in which the divine has felt the most distant and distracted, how might the Canaanite Woman's presence (then and now)—not a fix, not an answer to prayer, simply the assurance that you are never alone—make a difference?

6. What if you *could* imagine, *could* believe, *could* dare hope for the kind of advocacy that the Canaanite Woman demonstrates . . . and all on your behalf?

Chapter Nine: THE WOMAN AT THE WELL

Shame is the lie someone told you about yourself.
—Anais Nin

The final project of my master's degree was to distill three years of study into one singular takeaway *and* compellingly articulate my passion and heart moving forward. To say that I was overwhelmed by this task would not begin to capture it. I started listing possibilities, attempting to connect the dots between all that I'd learned with any modicum of relevance it might have beyond the classroom (a challenge, given that I'd been studying theology all this time!). I considered option after option, only to discard them for being too boring or too hard or too research-y or too "who cares?" Nothing seemed to land.

All the while, my mind kept wandering to a rudimentary hypothesis I'd been playing with. I was pretty sure there was a connection between the way in which the ancient, sacred stories of women had been told throughout time and the deepest struggles and pains women still felt today—individually, collectively, and culturally. But how could I prove it? Most of my "data" was in the realm of hunch and anecdote. I was horribly biased, my opinions wildly subjective. And I was convinced that I was right.

I needed a test case—one story with which to apply my theory. I decided on the Woman at the Well.

HER TEXT
—paraphrased from the Gospel of John, chapter 4

It's the middle of the day in the desert and the temperature is almost intolerable. A group of men travel along
a dusty road on the outskirts of town and come across
an ancient well. One of them—the leader it seems—sits
down to rest and sends the others ahead for food. When
a woman comes to the well to draw water, he asks her
for a drink. Conversation ensues—full of twists and
turns, questions asked, multiple topics covered. If you
could overhear them, you'd quickly recognize that they
are both wise, thoughtful, even witty. You might even
be convinced they are enjoying not only the banter but
also each other.

"How is it that you, a Jew, ask me, a Samaritan woman,
for a drink—especially given the history of animosity
between our people?"

"If you knew who it is that asks for a drink, you would
ask for one instead and receive living water."

"Well, that would be difficult, given that you have nothing to draw with and the well is deep. Are you greater
than our father Jacob, who gave us this well and drank
from it himself, along with his sons and his livestock?
And where does this living water come from, exactly?"

"Everyone who drinks the water from this well will be
thirsty again, but whoever drinks the water I give them
will never thirst again; instead, they will know a never-
ending spring of life within them."

"Sir, give me this water so that I won't get thirsty and have to keep coming to this well."

"Go, call your husband and come back."

"I have no husband."

"You have spoken the truth. In fact, you've had five husbands, and the man you are with now is not your husband."

"*Ahhhh*. I can see that you are a prophet. Tell me: why is it that you Jews insist that Jerusalem is the only place for worship, while we claim it is here on the mountain where our ancestors worshiped?"

"Dear woman, the time is coming when it won't matter where you worship—on the mountain or in Jerusalem. In fact, the time is here even now, when true worshipers will worship God in spirit and in truth."

"I know that the Messiah is coming. When he does, he will explain everything to us."

"I am he—the one speaking to you."

Just then, the man's disciples returned. They were surprised to find him talking with this woman. Still, none of them dared ask why he would do such a thing.

The woman left her water jar behind and ran back to town. She told everyone she could find, "Come, see a man who told me everything I ever did. Could this be the Messiah?"

Because of her, Samaritans streamed from the village to hear him speak—and when he did, they said to the woman, "Now we believe—not because of what you told us but because we have heard him ourselves. Now we know that he is, indeed, the one who will save us."

———— ⟨❁⟩ ————

ALMOST TWENTY YEARS HAVE PASSED since I wrote that thesis paper, but I dug it out recently, curious to see if what I articulated that long ago still holds water. If anything, I'm more compelled, more adamant, and more committed than I was even then—to the Woman at the Well herself, but also to how critical it is that these women's stories be reimagined and retold through *their* lens, not only on their behalf but also our own.

What I'd forgotten was that I'd rewritten this story completely from her perspective:

> A woman comes to the well in the heat of the day. She has been ostracized by the other women of the town because, in truth, they can choose no other response. She doesn't resent them. The rabbis have made it clear that a divorced woman is sinful and must be shunned. She knows they are acutely aware of how easily men can divorce their wives for the smallest of infractions, real or imagined. She knows, as do they, that she has never chosen divorce; few women ever do or could even if they wanted to. And had she been accused of adultery, the Mosaic Law would have required her death by stoning. But here she is—living, breathing, and drawing water at this well.
>
> She reminds the townswomen of how tenuous their safety truly is: they are easily dispensable—a commodity, at best a convenience. She reminds them of the whisper they sometimes hear within their own hearts—a distant recollection that they are strong, intelligent, and courageous, just like her. Most days, though, it's too painful for them to face, so they turn away. Knowing this doesn't make it any less painful for her. She is separated from women who were once her friends. She misses the conversations that only women have, the unspoken alliances that form through shared experiences. No matter how well she understands them, it still stings.

So, when she can, she converses with the men of the village. Her viewpoints and thoughts are trivialized—justified on the grounds that women are seen as inherently unwise and uninformed—but she employs all her intellect, humor, and wit regardless. She knows she is vulnerable to assault and consistently told she deserves it—her sexual presence a threat to male purity. She is a conundrum: both dangerous and desired.

Perhaps that is part of what enabled her five marriages. Even one divorce could leave a woman discarded, homeless, without resource or support. But men continue to wed her. She continues to survive. She is provocative, brilliant, and (secretly) admired by both the women and men who purport to shun her.

Lost in thought about all of this, she hardly notices she is no longer alone.

"May I have something to drink?"

She is used to men speaking to her and knows better than to assume they are truly interested in her or what she has to say; usually, they care only for what she has to offer. Why would today be any different? Instinctively, she shoots back a response from a place of highly honed defensiveness, "How is it that you, a Jew, ask water of me, a Samaritan woman?" But even as she asks the question, something is different. He isn't taunting her. He isn't staring at her, defying her to divert her eyes. He seems genuine, even tender and kind. Can she trust her intuition?

As their conversation proceeds, she realizes he is different from any man she's ever known. He is willing to hear her thoughts and isn't at all intimidated by what she knows about the history of this place, their common ancestors, their divergent takes on worship. He cares about what she has to say and even holds her gaze. And though if we were to overhear them it might sound like she is being evasive or trying to shift the focus of their dialogue, that is not it at all. She is actually being listened to and finally being heard! There is so much she wants to talk about that she can hardly stick to one topic. When he asks about her husband, she senses that his question is not to condemn but to compassionately acknowledge how dry and parched her life is, just like these desert sands in the middle of the day. For the first time, she is truly seen, heard, and understood. This man is different.

She begins to consider an incredible prospect; her mind spins as she recalls every detail she has ever heard about the promised Messiah. Could it be? But that would mean she is talking to him! That would mean that the promised redeemer sees *her* as worth hearing and knowing. And that moment of awareness changed everything.

His friends arrive on the scene, and although she is obliquely aware of their all-too-familiar disdain, she doesn't care. She holds a truth in her heart that cannot be taken from her, a possession that cannot be contained in a water jug. "Living water," he called it. Yes, that was what he has given her. She is refreshed; her endless, nameless thirst is quenched. And she sees herself through his eyes: a woman of value, of worth, of voice. Nothing will ever be the same again.

There was much more to the paper: historical and cultural context, quotes from academicians, theological argument, lots of footnotes. But when all of that is stripped away—then and now—the Woman at the Well stands squarely on her own. She always has. I can see, decades later, that when I named this, nothing was ever the same again . . . for me. Her story changed everything. *She* did. It's my hope (and horribly biased belief) that she'll change everything for you, too.

———— ❦ ————

THE STORY OF THE WOMAN AT THE Well was one I knew fluently growing up . . . just like Eve's. I knew exactly what it was about, the lesson to be extracted, and the obvious point: hers was a story of how *not* to be.

I knew the cultural custom was for women to draw the day's water in the early morning, far before the temperature rose; because she was there in the middle of the day, and alone, she was obviously unwilling to face anyone and ashamed. I knew her shame was appropriate, given the five husbands plus the "living in sin" situation. I knew she was shockingly impertinent to speak to Jesus as she did—evasive and constantly changing the subject. I knew he was only talking to her so that she would honestly (and finally) acknowledge her many sins—a testament to *his* character and graciousness in spite of her behavior. I knew this story wasn't about her; it was, *she* was, simply a prop to tell and glorify the story of a particular man.

Based on how I'd heard the story repeatedly told, any nagging questions I might have had didn't hold water. She *must* have felt shame, given that she came to the well in the middle of the day, right? All the other women would have been there hours earlier, while the sun was still low in the sky. Clearly, she didn't want to be seen or judged by them. She *definitely* felt shame when Jesus asked her to get her husband, right? He would have expected her to feel exactly that, given her story *and* the ample opportunity she had to come clean. To make matters worse, she kept changing the subject—unwilling to answer his questions. Shameful! She was *deserving* of shame, given that the disciples silently questioned why Jesus was talking with her, right? And given that the towns-people said, "Now we believe—*not* because of what you told us but because we have heard him for ourselves," they clearly judged her and found her undeserving of any credit whatsoever, right?

It was obvious: shame was the appropriate response to her life, repentance was clearly needed, and she was changed because of a man's (some would say God's) willingness to condescend.

If you think you hear just a *touch* of condescension in my own tone, you'd be right. The ease with which her shame rolls off the tongues of those who've told her story throughout time is embarrassing and sad. It infuriates me. And it breaks my heart. If we ever wonder why shame feels so damn familiar to us, the story of the Woman at the Well provides one of too many examples of just how pervasive and persistent its assumption is. Then, now, still. Erica Jong got it right when she said, "Show me a woman who doesn't feel guilty and I'll show you a man."[1]

Dr. Brené Brown defines shame this way:

Shame is the intensely painful feeling or experience of believing that we are flawed and therefore unworthy of love, belonging, and connection. [It] thrives on secrecy, silence, and judgment. If you put shame into a petri dish and douse it with these three things, it will grow exponentially into every corner and crevice of our lives.[2]

Shame is vicious. It eats away at us, shuts us down, and keeps us from fully participating in life. We stay in the shadows for fear of the light. Our backs bow for the weight of its burden. And the longer we carry it, the longer it gestates, the less deserving we feel of anything else, anything different, anything at all. After all, it's undoubtedly our fault to begin with—as Eve's story echoes yet again.

When I was in my twenties, I went through a string of relationships, if you could call them that. They were exciting and intense, but usually over before they began. I told myself that it was all worth it, that this endless compromise of my values and very self would pay off . . . eventually. Surely someone would come along and save me. Someone would see me for who I truly was, whisk me away to the life I'd imagined, and not only help me forget my past but also completely erase every painful emotion it summoned. On the outside, everything looked fine. I went to work. I smiled at strangers. I had pleasant conversations with my parents when I went home for the weekend every now and then. I went to church on Sundays, sang the hymns, took notes on the sermon, and vowed to do better, *to be better*. But on the inside, everything was dark. I suppressed my secrets, felt like a fraud, and was trapped in a shame spiral that sucked me into its centrifugal force.

By the end of my thirtieth year, things had finally turned the corner. I was married—and to a pastor, no less. By the time I turned forty my daughters were two and four, and I had started my master's degree in theology. Somehow—miraculously, I thought—I'd managed to put my past behind me, move on, and make a life for myself of which I was actually proud. I had escaped shame's grip . . . or so I thought.

It was in a psychology course that shame rushed back with a vengeance. The assignment was to chronicle my entire sexual history and corresponding beliefs about myself as result. It was excruciating to write, even more painful to turn in. My only saving grace was that the professor asked for a printed vs. electronic document along with his promise to return both the paper and a tape that held his recorded thoughts. I'll never forget his voice, let alone his words, in response to what I'd disclosed: *I wonder, Ronna, if you might consider your sexual history as a normal, even beautiful part of your story instead of a source of shame. It's possible, probable even, that it has made you who you are: passionate, full of desire, awake, alive, and profoundly relational.*

It would have *never* occurred to me to view my story, let alone myself, without shame. I was clear: when a woman exhibits any behavior outside the bounds of what is allowed, shame is the only and appropriate response. To *not* feel shame, to be shame*less*? That was even worse. But his question opened something up within me.

What if shame was never necessary for me to feel in the first place—ever? What if shame was *not* what others applied to my behavior (or would, if my secrets were known)? What if the divine did not impatiently wish that I would just be honest, repent, and finally turn my life around? What if, indeed?! That would mean that the burden I'd carried for years could be lifted. I would be cut loose from shame's oppressive weight and condemning presence. I could show up in my own life—nothing held back, nothing hidden or withheld, no part of me secreted away. Like the coolest drink of water on the hottest of days.

It would be two years later, in the final class of my degree, that I would turn all my attention to the Woman at the Well—that I would come to see her story as *my* own. *Not* a story of how *not* to be, as I'd learned over the years, but of a woman who offered me endless solidarity, support, and solace—a life that was *never* about shame. Even now, decades later, I can barely imagine the life I might have lived far sooner had I heard her story in a re-visioned and redeemed way from the start. She has been offering us this respite all along—waiting patiently to lift shame's burden, to erase it as our default and defining emotion. We just didn't know to turn to her, to listen to her, to see her as our dearest companion and most perfect mentor and muse. Now we do. She's worth another look, a closer look, and our endless gratitude.

———— ⟨⟫⟨⟫⟩ ————

WHEN WE LOOK CLOSER, HERE IS WHAT we see: there is *no* mention of shame *at all* in the story of the Woman at the Well. This feels worth repeating: there is *no* mention of shame *at all* in her story. It has been added by her storytellers throughout time. There is nothing that names it as what she definitively knew or experienced. There is no blatant evidence that others felt she should. And there is no reference that even slightly infers Jesus applied it to her. Every bit of the shame that this story has spoken of *ad nauseum* has been assumed—and then played on endless repeat.

How is it that centuries of interpretive work done by incredibly learned academicians and theologians has painted her almost exclusively with shame's broad brush? The simple answer, yet again, leads us back to Eve: shame is almost always the default attribution to a woman's will, her choices, or the slightest hint she might be living her story on her own terms. The more complicated answer is a combination of patriarchy, misogyny, cultural conditioning, and, undoubtedly, fear. And why?

Well, consider what it would have meant, even the very first time her story (let alone Eve's) was told if she was seen *without* a patina of shame. To honor her? To view her through a lens of distinction or grace? To encounter a woman who goes places on her own, who has the capacity to endure excruciating levels of loss and still love, who is smart enough to have brilliant conversations with a stranger (a *male* stranger, no less)? To let any of this stand would upend everything: the authority and stature of men—particularly religious/political leaders, prescribed roles within the home and larger community and, heaven forbid, women's reluctance to leave their marriages and "live in sin!"

We can smirk at all of this, of course, but what we're reacting to is a far deeper, painful, and angering truth: shame works. Hardly unique to a woman's experience in the ancient world, it persists, even flourishes, still. Women's sexual exploits are seen as shocking and unbelievable, while men's are barely mentioned, acceptably quieted, even completely ignored. "Boys will be boys" excuses bad behavior (in boys *and* men)—especially that which sexualizes women—while girls are called whores and disbelieved when they testify about their own sexual harm. President Bill Clinton is impeached then acquitted, while Monica Lewinsky becomes a social pariah for at least a decade of her life before rising out of the ashes, shedding the mantle of shame, and speaking out. Comedian Bill Cosby is released from prison even though more than fifty women made accusations of sexual assault and misconduct. It is allowed behavior to rake Ketanji Brown Jackson over the coals in Senate hearings in an attempt to discredit her qualifications as a Supreme Court Justice. The list goes on. The efficiency with which a man's choices become a woman's shame is mind-boggling.

It doesn't surprise me at all that this is the woman we've come to know in the story of the Woman at the Well, that shame has been added in after the fact and is part-and-parcel with how her story and she herself are seen and understood; how almost all women are. But not being surprised is a far cry from not being incensed. I *am* incensed.

———— ⌦⌫ ————

SHAME WAS *ADDED* TO THE STORY OF the Woman at the Well. So what was left out?

The common interpretive takeaway from her conversation with Jesus was that she was impertinent and evasive, and when things got personal, she intentionally changed the subject. Here's the (shaky) evidence: When he asked her for a drink, she questioned why he would do so. When he told her that she should be asking *him* for living water, she said, "Tell me where to get this water so that I never have to come to this well again!" When he told her to get her husband, she said she didn't have one. When he agreed, she then asked about the best and right place to worship. Their banter continued with her declaration of the someday-Messiah and his acknowledgment that he was exactly that. Amazing. But apparently every bit of this was her effort to skirt out from under what he was *actually* trying to say; no matter which direction he went, she detoured and derailed things—or so we're told. "[She is] characterized as one who has yet to feel pangs of conscience for her sins . . . she speaks rashly with Jesus because she is unaware of her own desperate condition. Jesus therefore uncovered the wounds of her sin, making her feel the guilt of her shameful crime . . ."[3]

I could not disagree more. Focusing on shame that *does not* exist in the text itself becomes an incredibly convenient way to forget—if not blatantly omit—what is most true about this woman: she is brilliant!

In all the Gospels (the New Testament accounts of Jesus's life), his conversation with her is the longest, the most intelligent, and certainly the most theological he has with *anyone*. If you're at all familiar with these texts, you know that Jesus frequently spoke in parables—short and pithy stories—so that people could better understand his ideas and beliefs. The questions most often asked were not based in curiosity but rather attempts to accuse and entrap him. And in an inventory of the conversations he had with men—specifically his disciples—he constantly had to re-explain things, make them simpler, to help them grasp his meaning. When juxtaposed with this story and the dialogue shared with the Woman at the Well, Jesus encounters someone closer to his equal than any other.[4] Her questions and responses demonstrated a knowledge that would have been, for the most part, off-limits to her gender. She was quick, witty, even funny. She didn't defer or feign ignorance (or express the least bit of shame). She did not demur and did not hold back. And she was highly curious, as anyone would be, about an endless spring of water.

I picture the two of them sitting side by side, completely delighted with each other. It would have been a profound experience for her—*finally* being seen and heard, allowed and respected, and especially by a man. It would have been a profound experience for him—*finally* talking to someone who could keep up, who was engaged, who asked good questions, who was interested and interesting.

Can you think of a single story in this text in which a woman so boldly and blatantly interacts with a man, let alone the divine? There *are* others, believe me; but just like the story of the Woman at the Well, they've not been told or honored. And in their absence, we have no way of knowing that we can do the same— that we *are* the same. The list of what this omission has cost us, what it has reinforced, and what it has led us to believe—and not believe—about our identity and worth as women is long. It has kept us from seeing ourselves, like her, as fully *deserving* of this kind of relationship with anyone and most especially the divine.

The Woman at the Well, fully aware of what has been added to her story throughout time and just as clear on what's been omitted, stands firm in who she knows herself to be and comes alongside us as our strongest supporter and most intimate friend. She gently reminds us that the shame we've carried is unnecessary—as unrealistic as that which has been attributed to her. She unabashedly affirms just how brilliant we are. She calls us to unapologetically express our opinions and beliefs, to step into contexts and conversations with the full expectation of being heard, appreciated, and enjoyed. And she promises to hear us herself—listening, responding, and expressing her heart on our behalf, healing our stories as hers has always warranted, and beckoning us into a life of bold, beautiful, expressed, and lived wisdom.

———————— ❦ ————————

LARGE SWATHS OF MY UNDERSTANDING of God were shaped by the usual telling of the Woman at the Well's story. I was convinced that I needed to repent, change, ask for "living water," and hope for eternal life. It would not have occurred to me that the interaction between this woman and this man could, in any way, mirror something redemptive or be an invitation to relationship with the divine, let alone be anything I could ever pray to experience or know. To even consider such a thing felt foreign, if not slightly blasphemous—impossible, if not a bit crazy.

Whether or not your history or heritage is like my own, the god in this story is probably *not* the god of whom you learned. Instead, he (definitely "he") is often personified as a white-bearded man who sits on high—distant, "above" us, all-seeing and all-knowing. In some doctrine, he showers gifts on those who honor him; wealth and prosperity are the expected markers of *our* goodness and holiness. In other systems of belief, it is an endless and tiring quest to somehow deserve his love; our shame, sin, and inherent weakness keep us humble, and we are clear about our need for his forgiveness. And still more view obedience to the law and upholding tradition as what merits God's favor and hastens his coming—whether for the first time or the last.

These are broad, sweeping generalities, of course. My intention is not to disrespect or disparage anyone's particular faith background or personal beliefs. Instead, I want to invite a provocative comparison between the stories we've inherited and held and what this woman's story demonstrates, even declares.

In the Woman at the Well's interaction with Jesus, we witness an experience with and of the divine that is distinct from much of what we've considered possible and nearly all of what we've been told and taught. She was spoken to directly—no pretense, no holding back, and certainly no intermediary. And all of this in the middle of the day, in the open—no shadow or shade of any kind. She asked questions and received clear replies. Questions were asked of her, and her answers were heard—no shame leveled or even insinuated. She was not wanted or "allowed" for what she could do or give, nothing was demanded of her, and she stood on equal footing with Jesus. Nor was she left guessing as to who he was: in one of only a handful of recorded times, he named (to a woman, no less) that he was, indeed, the Messiah.

And what of his experience of her? Far from impervious or aloof, *he* was impacted by her. He was engaged. One might even say he was *captivated*.

That is the man. But what of the divine? The Woman at the Well uniquely encountered a god who did not condemn. She conversed with a god who appreciated everything about her. She was seen and heard, honored and valued—perhaps for the very first time—with no prerequisites to meet, no worthiness to prove, and nothing taken from her, willingly or not. She was welcomed and wanted in the very best of ways. If we allow this to be true, our every expectation changes when it comes to interacting with the divine. It has the potential to heal every image and experience of God that has harmed. It offers us a breathtaking glimpse into the heart of the sacred—one we may otherwise rarely, if ever, come to know: this man/god delighted in *her*—exactly as she was, who she was, in that moment. *More than enough*.

Can you imagine it? *This* experience of the sacred? Being fully known and loved by the divine, with nothing required? A god who sees and honors us for who we are—distinctly as women? It's almost too good to be true, and a nearly foreign concept in light of "the God of our Fathers," the patriarchal god, the historical god, the male god. But it is *not* too good to be true when we re-vision and reimagine the stories of women, including that of the Woman at the Well.

The ancient, sacred stories of women invite us to an understanding of a god that is generous and compassionate. They reveal a god who delights in us. They enable us to see ourselves through the eyes of a god who applies no shame, no judgment, and no wrath, who instead honors our wisdom, delights in our desire, and celebrates all of who we are. The sacred stories of women heal us of imagery, concepts, and dogma—whether having to do with God, Spirit, the Universe, Love, or any number of names or ideologies—that have understandably and rightly caused us to distance ourselves from all of it.

WHEN I BEGAN WORKING WITH THE story of the Woman at the Well, I was still married to the pastor. I sat dutifully in the front row every Sunday morning with my adorable daughters. They were often in matching outfits, their little feet adorned with patent-leather shoes that dangled over the edge of the pew—the same feet that would run enthusiastically to Children's Church the second they were released from the formality of the "adult" service. When the hour drew to an end, I would take my husband's arm, walk down the aisle with him, and greet each person as they left—shaking hands, giving hugs, asking them how their week had been. Once back home, two pairs of patent-leather shoes now strewn across the floor, I thought about how hollow so much of it seemed. And when I was honest, I could admit that I didn't feel much different. None of this seemed right to me. Shouldn't the church be the very place in which we felt *most* alive, *most* engaged, *most* seen? Why was it just the opposite?

But something started, ever-so-slowly, to shift when I began to read and write between the lines of this woman's story. I listed out all the things I'd been told about her in one column, in the other, all that I discovered when I thought for myself. I inventoried all the ways I'd come to understand God with a capital G, even Jesus, compared to the way in which this man-and-Messiah showed up. I looked carefully at *why* her story had been told the way it had and began accounting for *everything* that would be different in my life and others' if it had been told from her perspective instead of with such a blatant agenda. And along the way, I *did* feel alive, engaged, and seen.

Those early days felt dangerous: retelling her story—even if only to myself—in any way other than how it had always been told, considering any god other than the only one I'd ever known. But the more I followed my heart (instead of distrusting it, as I'd been taught), the stronger my hunger grew. I longed for a god who would surprise me, shock me with intimacy and kindness, and not wield a single shard of shame. And Sunday mornings? I began to look intently into people's eyes as they filed out in numb but orderly fashion. I wondered how to invite them to a well on the side of a dusty road in the heat of the midday sun to have a conversation that would bring them back to life. What might they do with the story of a woman who knew their every thirst and a god who actually cared?

Maybe it *was* dangerous. Not too long after my exploration into this story and others began, the pastor and I divorced. I never stepped into that church again. Hardly any of the people I'd greeted every Sunday reached out. They wouldn't look me in the eye when we bumped into each other in the grocery store, at the girls' school, at community events. Some even sent me excruciating letters that accused me of being unkind, insensitive, and ungodly—definitely dangerous. But by that time, thankfully, the Woman at the Well was my closest companion—as was her god. Shame was no longer mine to believe, carry, or bear. And I knew that I had full permission to tell and live my story on my own terms.

The irony is not lost on me. In many ways, it was *exactly* the Woman at the Well's story—the shame-based version—that *kept* me in the marriage and the church, that kept me bound to a god who demanded my obedience and my endless striving to somehow be enough. The beauty is not lost on me either: it was a woman with five previous husbands and a current lover that *this god* chose to interact with. Apparently, a woman's marital status or lack thereof has no bearing on whom the divine chooses to talk with, accept, and be captivated by.

Most dangerous of all is recognizing and refuting just how profoundly our choices have been controlled by the way these stories have been told. But when the Woman at the Well is reconsidered, when all of these women's stories are rewritten and retold, we can do more than imagine a life in which we are more than enough, along with a god who encounters us in exactly the same way; we can live one.

———————— ❦ ————————

WE ARE OFTEN COMPELLED, IF NOT manipulated, by larger-than-life stories. We witness the before and after and wistfully watch the dramatic journey from being unloved to cherished and adored, from unknown to mind-bogglingly famous. And though I love a good rom-com or rags-to-riches tale as much as anyone, they often leave me feeling "less-than" and insignificant, bothered by a false and unrelenting belief that if only I had what they had, my life—*I*—would be better.

No. I want and need stories that are real. I want and need to be reminded that my normal, everyday life is sufficient and enough—that I am. And this is what I am given—what *we* are given—in the story of the Woman at the Well. She was imperfect. Her life was marked more by pain and loss than romantic bliss and wild success. But even so, or maybe even because of that, she was seen, heard, honored, and esteemed in the midst of *her everyday life*, not a miraculously transformed one.

This offers me tremendous hope. She does. There is nothing more I need aspire toward, nothing more I need to do, nothing more I need to try, nothing more I need to fix, nothing more I need to buy, nothing more I need to change. Perhaps there never was. Perhaps *my* everyday life has always been enough—worthy of being seen, heard, honored, and esteemed. And perhaps every bit of this has always been mine to acknowledge for myself—no miraculous transformation required, even wanted.

Oh, how we need the Woman at the Well's story in a world that inundates us with so many that serve no purpose other than convincing us of our lack. She offers us an infinite well of inspiration and a template for what real life looks like, filled to the brim and even overflowing with meaning, impact, and the sacred. She walks with us in *our* everyday life to remind us of just how worthy we are and always have been.

May it be so.

Dear One:

How many hours, days, weeks, months, and years have you searched for something, anything, that would quench your thirst, soothe your ragged breath, calm your restless heart, and ease your shame? If you're anything like me (which I know you are), your answer is "countless times, infinitely, and endlessly." All to little avail.

In one unexpected encounter with the divine, I discovered a well that would never run dry—not outside of me (as I'd been certain it was), but within. I saw, once and for all, that I was worthy of love, brilliant beyond compare, and devoid of all shame.

That same well is yours. Drink deep. And walk through your world aware that shame is never yours to carry or bear. Set it all down and don't turn back. Turn your face toward the new story that awaits you as my daughter, my lineage, my kin.

QUESTIONS FOR
FURTHER REFLECTION:

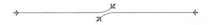

1. "If we ever wonder why shame feels so damn familiar to us, the story of the Woman at the Well provides one of too many examples of just how pervasive and persistent its assumption is." If you were already familiar with this story before reading this chapter, was shame the default you knew and understood? In what ways has that impacted what you've believed about yourself and your own story?

2. Have you ever considered viewing yourself and your story without shame? What if you could?

3. What do you make of the fact that there is no mention of shame in the Woman at the Well's story—that, rather, this element has been added by her storytellers throughout time?

4. When you consider the possibility that Jesus was captivated by her brilliance and loved every minute of their conversation together, what does that bring up for you? Where do you resist to the possibility that such a thing could be true between you and the divine?

5. We are so often tempted by dramatic and aspirational stories. They often cause us to second-guess and dismiss the significance of our own; they keep us on an endless treadmill of needing to do more, change more, be more. How has that made itself manifest in your life?

6. What respite might you experience with the imperfect and "real" story of the Woman at the Well? What if it is in the midst of your everyday life that you are most seen, heard, honored, and esteemed—not only by the divine but by your own self?

Chapter Ten: THE WOMAN
OF REVELATION 12

*She is so bright and glorious that you cannot look at her
face or her garments for the splendor with which she shines.
For she is terrible with the terror of the avenging light-
ning, and gentle with the goodness of the bright sun; and
both her terror and her gentleness are incomprehensible
to humans. . . . But she is with everyone and in everyone,
and so beautiful is her secret that no person can know the
sweetness with which she sustains people and spares them
in inscrutable mercy.*
—HILDEGARD VON BINGEN

Of all the stories I reimagine and retell, this one *always* has
me in tears. I'm not completely sure why. I have a few
ideas, of course—and I'll explore them in the pages that follow—
but none of them quite capture the way that she captures me.
Maybe it's picturing her. Maybe it's that she's basically unknown
and unacknowledged. Maybe it's the relatable aspects of her fear
and pain. Maybe it's her fight. Undoubtedly, it's all of these and
then some.

Isn't this the way of every and any woman's story that moves
us? It summons something within us that calls us up, forward,
on, into, out of, beyond. Just in being heard, it reminds us of who
we are; it reveals, yet again, all the ways in which the world has

worked to make us forget this truth. It invites us to more—more possibility, more potential, more voice, more courage, more self.

If I had to choose only one story that would offer me all of this and then some, I would choose the Woman of Revelation 12.

She's had an uphill battle in being known and honored, seen, and heard . . . if she has been at all. The text that surrounds her is filled with allegory, metaphor, and myth-like creatures. There are swords, battles, and blood. There are thrones, tears, and talk of triumph. We would never read it to children, and it's rarely read by adults. It's confusing, a bit scary, and far easier ignored. For many who *have* read it, especially voices in more conservative camps, it is seen as a warning—a prediction of the end of the world, filled with signs that prove we are (nearly) there, evidence of the Messiah's imminent return before we're faced with hell or heaven. And if all this weren't enough, her story is almost at the end of the bible itself; few make it that far!

I cannot recall how I stumbled across her in the first place; it is not a story I was told over and over like Eve's. But once I found her—or better said, once she found me—I was gripped, and I have been ever since.

Wading through the strangeness of her text feels almost intentional—as though she's been lying in wait, hiding out within pages and paragraphs that few have dared to enter or even bother with. Her story is like discovering a treasure chest—buried and almost forgotten. When she *is* discovered, seen, and honored, we uncover what she's been trying, all along, to reveal: *we* are the treasure. But just like her, we have gotten lost in texts and translations, stories and messages, that have kept *us* obscured, hidden, and unable to shine. Until now . . .

Her Text
—paraphrased from Revelation, chapter 12

A great sign appeared in heaven: a woman clothed with the sun, the moon under her feet, and she wore a crown of twelve stars on her head. She was pregnant and cried out in the pain of labor.

Another sign appeared in heaven: an enormous red dragon with seven heads and ten horns and seven crowns on its heads. Its tail swept a third of the stars out of the sky and flung them to the earth. It stood before the woman, prepared to devour her child the moment it was born.

She gave birth to a son who, as it had been foretold, would one day rule all the nations. God rescued the child from the dragon—whisked him away to safety. The woman was kept safe as well. She fled into the wilderness to a place prepared for her by God, where she might be taken care of for 1,260 days.

Then war broke out in heaven. Michael and his angels fought against the dragon and won. He was hurled to the earth, his angels with him—that ancient serpent called the devil, or Satan, who leads the whole world astray.

When the dragon saw that he had been defeated, he pursued the woman. She was given the two wings of a great eagle so that she could fly to the place prepared for her in the wilderness, where she would be taken care of for a time, times and half a time, out of the dragon's reach. The dragon spewed water like a river from its mouth, trying to sweep her away with the torrent. But this time the earth itself rose up on her behalf by opening its mouth and swallowing the river. At this the dragon, even more enraged, went off to wage war against the rest of the woman's offspring. . . .

———— ⟨⊙⟩ ————

THE WOMAN OF REVELATION 12 IS A full-circle return to Eve. From a creation story that began in utter darkness (and has remained painfully shrouded in the same) to one that is ablaze with radiant light. From a woman in stitched-together leaves to one who is clothed with the sun, has the moon at her feet, and wears a crown of twelve stars on her head. She is Eve's redemption, a mirror of who Eve always was, someone we've lost sight of along the way: unique, distinct, and awe-inspiring. There is nothing and no one like her, like either of them. When linked together, beginning and end, alpha and omega, they reveal womankind as we were always intended, as we always have been: impossible to ignore, sovereign, and glorious.

It feels to me that this text has always had a mind of its own—resolutely determined that Eve and all women throughout time be seen accurately and honored profoundly before the final page was turned. The Woman of Revelation 12 sets everything right, gets the last word, and defeats any force or foe that would attempt to tell a different tale. In doing so, she calls us to the destiny that has always been ours. She boldly declares that the final page has *not* yet been turned in our story, that *this* is the way ours has always been meant to be told: mythic, regal, bringing forth life, and undefeated. Hardly the stuff of fairy tales, but true and real and ours to believe, claim, and live.

IN EVERY PREVIOUS CHAPTER, I'VE BEEN able to name the ways in which the woman's story has been *told* and how that has impacted us—most often for ill. I cannot do that with this story: for one, it's rarely been told at all; second, there is very little in this text with which storytellers or interpreters have taken issue over time. Were I to guess, it's because it has baffled them as well.

Who is she?

She is unprecedented. "The most frequent reference is to Mary, the mother of Jesus, and many works of art portray this woman as the Madonna with child."[1] Also present, though, is the obvious-and-significant influence of ancient goddesses: Isis with her son, Horus; Inanna with the moon at her feet; even Gaia, present in imagery of the earth itself.

Who is she?

She is unparalleled. There is no other story of a woman in this text that allows for this much sovereignty, this much beauty, this much divine protection, this much gloriousness. Perhaps *this* is the primary reason we have not heard of her: were we to know and honor *this woman* as one from whom we descend, no dragon—let alone the powers that be, the patriarchy, or any "labor" we might know—could stop us either.

Who is she?

She is undefeatable. No matter her pain or fear, no matter what confronts her, no matter how she is pursued, she is miraculously (and rightfully) cared for by God, even by the earth itself, as is her child.

Who is she?

She is the mythic, epic, one-of-a-kind image of who all women truly are, of who *you* are: unprecedented, unparalleled, and most definitely undefeatable.

ONE MORNING, SHORTLY AFTER MY marriage ended, I drove the girls to before-school care as they sobbed uncontrollably in the backseat: *"Why do you have to go to work? Please stay with us, Mom! Just today. Just this once, okay? Pleeeeeease!"* It took every bit of will I had to peel them off my arms and legs, sign them in, then turn and walk away. I barely made it back to the car, unsure of how I would survive the hour-long commute to work, not to mention the eight hours ahead and second hour-long trip I would have to bear before seeing them again.

That afternoon, heading back to them through traffic and tears, I wondered why I ever thought I could create some semblance of a life beyond my marriage. I wasn't sure what had possessed me to think I had the right to make a decision on my own behalf. I questioned my sanity at birthing them in the first place; even more, questioned how I would ever manage to raise them to be responsible adults who still wanted to speak to me, let alone appreciated and loved me for what I believed I was doing *for them*. Doubt reigned supreme. My inner critic was on overdrive. The self-contempt was nearly all-consuming. I felt small, afraid, and broken. It was as though I was standing at the edge of some deep, dark chasm into which all three of us were surely going to fall.

As I willed my heart rate to a semi-normal state and tried to let my red-rimmed eyes begin to recover, the Woman of Revelation 12 came to mind. I reminded myself of her story as best I could— and started crying again, but this time for a very different reason. Suddenly I was not quite so alone. I felt a strange sort of support that summoned a strength within me I'd not known was mine to draw upon. I *literally* felt my posture change. And as I looked into my tear-filled eyes in the rearview mirror, I swear I caught a glimpse of a crown. By the time I arrived at the girls' after-school care, I felt steady and sure.

When I tucked them into bed that night, I told them a story about a woman who was clothed with the sun, had the moon at her feet, and wore a crown of twelve stars on her head. About how she was afraid, just like them. About how she was carried on the wings of an eagle to a place that helped her feel strong again. About how she'd give them eagle's wings too, so that they could fly with her over amazing deserts and beautiful mountains and winding rivers. About how she was with them all the time—fighting "dragons" imagined and real. About how they were just like her: that beautiful, that celestial, that powerful, and always, always kept safe.

That bedtime story was for me. I needed it. I needed her. I still do.

Thankfully, miraculously, the Woman of Revelation 12 returns again and again. The two of us talk of labor and birth, of fear and dragons, of eagle's wings and the earth's protection, of being goddesses together. And always, *always*, the light in the room seems to brighten. It could be my crown, I suppose—the stars sparkling. Maybe it's the glare that reflects off my sunlit robe or the way my shoes take on the glow of the moon. Whatever it is, I stand taller, breathe deeper, and remember, yet again, who I *truly* am: her daughter, her lineage, her kin.

———— ❦ ————

ALL WOMEN KNOW THE PAIN OF LABOR. It does not matter if it comes when bringing another human into the world or a painting, a delicious meal, a blog post, a piece of jewelry, a screenplay, or a book. All women, too, know the fear that accompanies every one of these births. *Will what I bring into the world survive and thrive? What lies in wait that threatens to devour?*

I have birthed two daughters and can attest to the pain and the fear, but I know almost exactly the same emotions when it comes to my writing. *Will what I have labored to bring forth be able to breathe? Will it live? Or does something dark and sinister yet wait to devour my words, my beliefs, my heart?* And unlike my pregnancies—knowing I could not forestall labor indefinitely— when it comes to putting my words on the page, I *can* hold them back for an eternity.

The birthing of ourselves into the world—whether through our creativity, through opening ourselves to love, through raising our voices, and/or through believing in our own value and worth—*can* be prevented and withheld. Which is why we so desperately need the story of the Woman of Revelation 12.

She knows what we are afraid of. She knows what it feels like to be on the precipice of bringing something magnificent into the world *and* crying out in the pain of labor. She knows the terror of all that overwhelms when we acknowledge what *is* ours to birth into the world—all that we've been nurturing, even sheltering, for such a long time. To let it see the light? To bring it outside of ourselves and into the world? To expose it to the "dragons" of others' opinions and thoughts? She knows just how scary and daunting every bit of this is. She also knows there is more to the story than this—both hers and ours.

———— ⟨⟩ ————

No sooner does the Woman of Revelation 12 birth her precious child than God swoops in and carries it to safety. Why? Because she is deserving of protection . . . as is her child. The very thing you most long to bring forth is also safe. Why? Because *you* are deserving of protection . . . as is your creation, your every expression, and your fullest self.

Chances are high, however, that you can look back at too many times in which this has not been the case—whether for you or those you know and love. Too many times when no god has swooped in, no protection has been forthcoming, and no safety has been offered or known.

Chances are high that the Woman of Revelation 12 would say the same. Having her newborn taken from her upon delivery was hardly an "answer to prayer." Why didn't God just slay the dragon so she could remain with her son? Why couldn't God offer care in ways that didn't require her heartbreak?

I cannot answer these questions, but I am relatively certain that the god we witness in this woman's story never intended anything less than her protection, safety, and wholeness. And I'm relatively certain that the same applies to my story—and yours. This hardly means we won't know fear or pain, that everything will make sense, that happy endings are guaranteed. But it might mean that the Woman of Revelation 12 calls us to trust that her god sees, understands, and even provides for us in ways that don't make sense *and* are no less powerful and true for that seeming lack of logic.

I love the possibility of this.

I also struggle with it.

The god I learned to believe in promised to provide for me on what seemed a conditional basis: *if* I was faithful, *if* I confessed my sins, *if* I did everything in my power to be good enough, worthy enough, perfect enough, repentant enough—enough, period. Granted, that's not what the text or even the doctrine (in its purest form) said, but it was definitely the subliminal message. So, when bad things happened—hard things, traumatic things, frightening things, excruciating things—I very quickly assumed it was my fault. I'd not held up my end of the bargain.

This makes me horribly sad: the legion of beliefs that kept me exhausted and feeling so, so alone. Even though I've long since left the god of shoulds and musts and have-tos, I still feel ambivalent. I still wonder what God is up to and how to make sense of it—especially when things are not going as I think they should and wish they would. I question if God exists at all. I ask myself if it matters—holding on to a belief in God. There are more days than not in which my honest answer is no.

But there are other days when the Woman of Revelation 12 comes to mind and heart and I am compelled by a god who defies all questions, all answers, *and* invites me to wonder, to magic, to the miraculous, to the incomprehensible; a god who sees me as glorious, radiant, and sovereign, just like her; a god who *does* swoop in, honor, and protect all that I birth into the world.

If I'm going to believe—whether every day or just some of them—this *is* the god I want. And it's exactly the god we witness in this woman's story (and every one I've told within this book): a god who has no prerequisites or demands; who endlessly and always shows up; who honors, serves, protects, and loves.

THERE IS SOMETHING ABOUT THE trifecta of women, deserts, and the divine that deserves our rapt attention.

Hagar runs away to the desert—and it is there that God shows up in visible form for the first time ever.

The Woman at the Well draws water in the desert's heat—and it is there that Jesus engages with her in the most powerful and honoring of ways.

The Woman of Revelation 12 cries out in a desert of pain and fear—and it is there that God not only rescues her but provides her comfort and restoration.

The same has been true for me. The deserts in which I've felt the most desperate and alone like Hagar, the most unseen and unheard like the Woman at the Well, and certainly the most exhausted and afraid like the Woman of Revelation 12 are those in which the divine has consistently shown up on my behalf.

I would love to tell you that I've recognized this in the moment, that I've always been grateful, that I've never known a moment of doubt. A truer statement would be that I've resisted it all; I've longed for anything other than the desert's excruciating heat. Still, with hindsight and without exception, I have been nurtured, cared for, even carried in the driest and most desolate of days, seasons, and experiences. At times this succor has come through others—their presence, kindness, and truth-telling. Other times it has come through unexplainable coincidences or serendipities. And it has certainly been mine through the sacred stories of women—finding myself within them and being found by them. I'm slightly loath to admit it, but the desert *is* where I've encountered myself and God in the most honest and intimate of ways.

Still, even so, I resist—the desert, the smallest hint of suffering, struggle, or hardship, and, yes, the god who seems to dwell there more than anyplace else. The Woman of Revelation 12 is who draws me back to the desert's arid sands again and again. She takes my hand and nearly pulls me along. And as I reacclimate to the heat, I hear myself say, "I belong here. This is the land I have been looking for all my life, though I never knew it till now." To which she responds, "Come further up, come further in!"[2]

She is right: we must go further into her story to understand why the desert is far from a place to avoid; is, in fact, just the opposite. Yes, there is the pain of labor. Yes, there is the fear as a dragon threatens. But it is what happens next that makes all the difference for her and for us.

Let's return to the text:

> She gave birth to a son who, as it had been foretold, would one day rule all the nations. God rescued the child from the dragon—whisked him away to safety. The woman was kept safe as well. She fled into the wilderness to a place prepared for her by God, where she might be taken care of for 1,260 days.

It's significant and shocking (though not all that surprising) that we've missed this, that she's barely been spoken of, that such powerful advocacy and care has not been affirmed and named *on our behalf*. Instead, we have wandered through centuries, generations, and the most parched of deserts—have been denied her story and any sense of a god who not only fiercely protects women but loves them in profoundly unique and powerful ways.

When the Woman of Revelation 12 is honored and *her* god becomes the one we both expect and experience, *everything changes*. The desert is no longer ours to endure or suffer through but is instead the very place in which we are restored and reign— clothed with the sun, the moon at our feet, a crown of twelve stars on our head, and bringing forth life that will *not* be ignored.

———— ⟨☙⟩ ————

ONE OF MY VERY FAVORITE SCENES IN the movie version of *The Lord of the Rings* is when Arwen races through the forest on horseback to keep Frodo safe from the Ringwraiths—evil, life-less souls who tirelessly pursue the ring he carries. She narrowly escapes their grasp by crossing a river, but when the Ringwraiths and their horses enter in pursuit, she defiantly shouts, "If you want him, come and claim him!" Then in Elvish, she whispers, "*Nín o Chithaeglir lasto beth daer; rimmo nín Bruinen dan in Ulaer!*"—at which point torrents of water cascade down the valley and drown the evildoers in the rapids.

I cry at this scene—every time. I am undone by her confidence, her strength, and her ability to summon the earth itself to her will. She is beautiful and defiant and regal. She is so much like the Woman of Revelation 12. This probably explains why I cry at these verses—every time—as well:

> When the dragon saw that he had been defeated, he pursued the woman. She was given the two wings of a great eagle so that she could fly to the place prepared for her in the wilderness, where she would be taken care of for a time, times and half a time, out of the dragon's reach. The dragon spewed water like a river from its mouth—trying to sweep her away with the torrent. But this time the earth itself rose up on her behalf by opening its mouth and swallowing the river.

I am undone by *this* story and the woman within it. She is beautiful and defiant and regal as she cries out in labor. When pursued by a dragon, she flies on the wings of an eagle to safety. And when the dragon persists, the earth itself is summoned. I can almost hear her say, "If you want me, come and claim me!"

I have thought a lot about why both of these scenes captivate me. The best I can come up with is that something within me knows they are a glimpse of who I have the capacity to be, who I truly am. I'm not witnessing something fantastical or far away but rather something close by, close in, real, and true.

I conveniently forget every bit of this, though, on days in which I'd rather stay buried under the covers. Morning-noon-nights of being a mom, meal after meal of chicken nuggets, loads of laundry, endlessly cleaning up, failed attempts at patient listening, answering question after question, more cleaning. A long day of meetings in which I feel small and unseen or loud and out of line. An inevitable conversation that I am certain will go badly. Walking through all this and more while my own internal demons (and dragons) rage. I'm a long, long way from beautiful and defiant and regal.

Which is exactly why I *must* remember, why her story matters so very much. Not to somehow escape what's tedious, defeating, hard, and scary, but to step forth and reign. The Woman of Revelation 12 is my closest ally—especially on the days I want to stay in bed. She reminds me that I am just like her: I cry out, am afraid, feel pain, and am exhausted and weary and spent. She reminds me that just like her, I am not alone: she stands with me in the labor, in the battles, in the wilderness, and as the very earth rises up in solidarity and strength. And as I finally stumble to the mirror and see little to nothing that resembles the sun, the moon, or a star-studded crown, I hear her say: "Remember who you are: my daughter, my lineage, my kin."

———— ⟪◦⟫ ————

WHILE I WAS WRITING ABOUT VASHTI, there were rumors of *Roe v. Wade* being overturned. But now, as I come to the final pages of this book, I have just heard the news: the Supreme Court *did* overturn the decision. I am enraged. I am gutted. And though I can hardly see through my tears, I search for something, anything to say to my daughters about the reality in which they are forced to live. This is text I sent:

> *I am heartbroken on your behalf. I can only pray that you will somehow be able to sustain your own hope and joy in a world that is so dark and ignorant and violent. I love you both so very much.*

I can hardly bear to keep writing, to attempt any organization of my words and sentences on the screen, to think that I could possibly capture a cogent thought. It feels ridiculous and futile to have spent all these pages talking about how these women's stories have been told and the harm that has caused when it so blatantly persists. I can't see how any of it can possibly matter in a nation that refuses to enforce gun control but demands (and takes) control over women's bodies. Were I not so near the end of this book, the temptation would be strong to delete it in its entirety.

Then I see it. A single sentence I hastily typed a few days ago, a reminder I left for myself about how to end this chapter, a final takeaway from the Woman of Revelation 12:

> *She is restored so that she can return to the battle.*

And now, even more tears. I am humbled and undone. Of all the stories I've been working with, of all the things I've written, of all the notes I've left for myself, *this* is what shows up on this day, in this moment, right now.

She is restored so that she can return to the battle.

I do not know how to explain or understand this as anything but miracle, validation, and proof that these women continue to speak, remain present on my behalf, and faithfully offer me *exactly* the wisdom, blessing, and hope I most need. They *have restored me so that I can return to battle*—just like the Woman of Revelation 12. All I can hope is that my telling you this part of her story will help you to do the same.

So, through my tears (and a now-found box of Kleenex), these final thoughts . . .

I wish the Woman of Revelation 12's story ended with 1,260 days at a desert spa after flying on the wings of an eagle and being advocated for by the earth itself. But as is almost always true in our lives, so in hers: there is no happily-ever-after—at least not the one we might expect and hope. Her story ends with this line: "At this the dragon, even more enraged, went off to wage war against the rest of the woman's offspring. . . ."

It is a bold interpretive leap on my part, but I am certain I am right: She is carried into the wilderness for a time, times, and half a time so that she can gather the strength she needs. That same damn dragon is now pursuing her other daughters and sons. Vacation's over. Her sword is drawn. She will *not* be defeated. She will *not* let any harm come to those whom she has birthed, to all those she loves. *She is restored so that she can return to the battle.*

And of course, *of course*, she invites us to exactly the same.

Here at the very end of this sacred text (and even this book), the Woman of Revelation 12 embodies what every one of these women's stories have been saying all along—what they have been whispering, speaking, and shouting on our behalf throughout all of time: *We fight for you, we draw our swords, we stay in the battle, and we continue to whisper, speak, and shout so that you will know and trust that you are never alone when you are called to do the same.*

These women and their stories restore us so that we can stay in the battle that *still* persists—for all that we desire, all that we deserve, and on behalf of *our* daughters, *our* lineage, *our* kin.

May it be so.

Dear One:

I hear your cries—the pain of your labor. And I know your fear—your worry that all you have worked for, carried, and sheltered will surely be taken from you, even devoured. But that is not to be your fate. You are protected. You are cared for. You are whisked to safety. And not just you but all that you love, as well.

Take my hand. Claim the story that has always been yours to know and live. Step regally, royally, and powerfully into the honor and advocacy you have always deserved. The sun waits to clothe you in golden warmth. The moon gazes up at you with adoration. And the crown I wear belongs to you—its twelve stars embracing you in radiance and love. No dragon could possibly defeat you, a woman for whom both the divine and the earth itself will fight until the end of time.

So soar, dear one, on the wings of eagles. And as you do, remember who you are: my daughter, my lineage, my kin.

QUESTIONS FOR
FURTHER REFLECTION:

1. Can you imagine the Woman of Revelation 12 as a bedtime story? Who might you be today if you'd heard of her when you were young? And now that you have? What vision of your truest and most regal self does she awaken within you?
2. Do you feel the same fear I do when you consider birthing something into the world?
3. Can you imagine a god who sees you as glorious, radiant, and sovereign—a god who swoops in to honor and protect all that you birth into the world? What would that make possible? What would you attempt, risk, or create if you believed in such a god?
4. "I'm slightly loath to admit it, but the desert *is* where I've encountered myself and God in the most honest and intimate of ways." Would you agree? What do you appreciate or resist in this possibility?
5. *She is restored so that she can return to the battle.* What does this look like for you—what does it invite, what does it mean?

Chapter Eleven:
A CHORUS OF VOICES

. . . our ancestors continue.
I have seen them.
I have heard their shimmering voices
singing.
—LUCILLE CLIFTON

D espite limiting myself to ten stories in these pages, there are so many more to tell—so many more women to honor, and so many more who honor you! Perhaps I will yet write of them, but for now, take in the names of just a few of the countless women who make up the chorus of voices that supports you and sings over you:

Sophia
Noah's Wife
Leah
Rachel
Rebekah
Miriam
The Pharaoh's Daughter
Lot's Wife
Abigail

Tamar
Dinah
Ruth
Jephthah's Daughter
Rahab
Deborah
Jezebel
Job's Wife
Delilah
Bathsheba
The Woman from the Song of Songs
Mary
Elizabeth
Jairus' Daughter
The Hemorrhaging Woman
The Unaccused Woman
Tabitha
Anna
Martha
Lois
The Women at the Tomb
Mary Magdalene

A chorus of voices, indeed.

The church my ex-husband pastored had an Easter Sunday tradition: after the sermon, the offering, all the things, an invitation was extended to join the choir onstage for the well-known chorus from Handel's Messiah. You can picture it, I'm sure: some folks in their choir robes, others in jeans, still more in fancy dresses and hats; every age, from the most senior of seniors to the youngest of children were represented in the crowd. Sheet music was handed out as the organ began to play the opening lines. Some read it diligently, barely looking up to see the choral director. Others were confident and clear on their part, having performed it many, many times. Regardless of their approach, when the growing crescendo of Hallelujah's began, I'd watch as, without fail, every face lit up. Whether on key or not, every person there sang as loudly as they possibly could—completely unselfconscious, fully present, fully alive. Somehow, despite the range in talent (or lack thereof), it was perfect. Perfectly human. Perfectly divine. It undid me every time.

I never joined them. Instead, I chose to stay seated, to witness the spectacle, to revel in the swell of volume and heart, to wipe away the tears that fell every single year as if on cue.

Despite having left the church nearly two decades ago, this memory touches a deep-rooted and tender place within me. There is something about the tradition, the music, the liturgy, and a gathered community of disparate souls that rises above all the doctrine and dogma, the harm, the biases, the arguments, and all that more often divides than unites.

And it gives me even the slightest taste of what it looks and feels like to be sung over by the ancient, sacred women whose stories I reimagine, retell, and rewrite—a gorgeous, breathtaking, and magnificent chorus of voices that call us up onstage, that refuses to let us to remain anonymous in our seat. They encircle us, arms around each other's waists, swaying to the rhythm. You can picture it, I'm sure: Women from the beginning of time right up to the present, clothed in the gowns and garb of their own history. No sheet music required; this is a song they have been singing since the day we were born. What are those words? Ah, yes—"You are our daughter, our lineage, our kin. . . ." Their faces light up, they sing as loudly as they possibly can, and they honor just how perfectly human we are—how perfectly divine, how immensely loved.

And, yet again, I am undone.

A chorus of voices. Every one of them—all of them together—are close in, ever-present, and always, *always* with you. You are *never* alone. So step up onstage, sing, shine, choose, desire, lead, speak, shout, say yes, say no, reign, demand, write, fight, love, change everything! *This is your story.* Yours to tell and live, to reimagine and rewrite, to claim as your own.

May it be so.

Afterword: REWRITING YOU— CLAIMING YOUR SACRED STORY AS YOUR OWN

This is our story to tell. You'd think for all the reading I do,
I would have thought about this before, but I haven't. I've
never once thought about the interpretative, the story telling
aspect of life, of my life. I always felt like I was in a story,
yes, but not like I was the author of it, or like I had any say
in its telling whatsoever.

—JANDY NELSON

I trust that as you have read of Eve, the Woman of Revelation 12, and every woman in between; you have experienced countless ways in which they have impacted, and continue to impact, your story for good and for ill. I trust that as I have named how each has been told throughout time, the influence those tellings have had on us and our world, and certainly all that is ours to claim when we reimagine them, that you have recognized your invitation to do the same. This *is* what these ten women (and I) long for on your behalf: a reimagining and rewriting of the stories that are yours, a living of the stories you desire and deserve.

It is a life's work to detach from and deconstruct any story that does you harm and to step into those that reveal and honor the divine within. It is a journey, a process, and a practice to consistently and bravely name the stories you've been told and the ones you tell yourself. It is a defiant and hope-filled act to reclaim them . . . and this time, on your own terms. Not just once, but repeatedly.

May it be so.

WHAT FOLLOWS IS A TEMPLATE, A MAP, a guide for you to carry with you as you endlessly and extravagantly rewrite *you*. Use it loosely. Apply every bit of your imagination, intuition, and brilliance. Know that you can't possibly get it wrong. Always, always, extend yourself infinite amounts of grace. And remember that you are never alone in any of this, because you are accompanied and companioned by every woman who has ever gone before. A chorus of voices, indeed. They sing over you. They stand with you. And they hand you the pen.

> *Every word a woman writes changes the story of the world, revises the official version.*
> —CAROLYN SEE[1]

Be curious about, name, and acknowledge the stories you've been told:

1. What stories did you hear as a child? What were the bedtime stories you were told at night? What were the earliest books you read or movies you watched? What were the messages—explicit and subliminal—that you automatically learned around your kitchen table, in the car, from family? What stories were told of relatives and friends, the black sheep or the rebels? (And were these stories praised or shamed?) What stories were you told and *not told* about relationships, conflict, money, appearance, body, success, religion, faith, and love?

2. List them all out: Cinderella, Snow White, Hansel and Gretel; Eve, Abraham, and Mary; Persephone, Carrie Bradshaw, and Hermione Granger. The aunt no one talks about. The neighbor everyone does. The divorce. The abandonment. The diets. The church. Considering these stories, what were the predominant messages or takeaways you absorbed and understood from each one? What was the motif or moral

of each story? What was the role and experience of women, specifically, in these stories?

3. Remember that little of this was ever conscious—was, instead, the water in which you swam. Be gentle as you excavate. Extend yourself grace as you look back. Hold memories loosely. Be willing to go deep. Know that you can come up for air at any time. Respite and rest are always yours.

Stories can break the dignity of a people. But stories can also repair that broken dignity.
—CHIMAMANDA NGOZI ADICHIE[2]

Inventory and reflect on how these stories have become the ones you tell yourself:

1. How have each of the messages and takeaways from these stories appeared in your own life, your own story? Be specific. Where and when have you believed them most, followed them blindly, known their harm, hoped for their happy ending?

2. How have the primary "lessons" in these stories been translated or morphed into your inner critic, the caustic voice you hear within, the standard of comparison by which you determine your value and worth?

3. When you hear the dialogue in your head, especially when it revolves around self-contempt or fear, what story can you connect this back to? Is it true or *simply* the story you've been told?

4. There is no shame, no matter what. Hear the voice of Eve, the Woman at the Well, even the divine: you are whole and complete, beautiful and deserving, worthy and wise beyond belief.

Once our old stories have been told, we need to find and claim the new stories which will inspire us to move forward.

It took me a long time to find my own guiding stories: stories which not only captured my imagination but which reminded me that there are other ways of belonging to the world than those that were handed down to me.
—SHARON BLACKIE[3]

Determine, dream, and defiantly step into the story you desire:

1. Beyond the promised happily-ever-after of fairy tales and certainly our culture, what do you really want? What do you most deeply desire? Nothing is out of bounds or off limits here. Let yourself name what your wild heart longs for most.
2. Acknowledge just how hard it is to desire. How risky. How brave. Give yourself space and time to ask these questions again and again: "What do I want?" "If I had it, what then?" "What's underneath?" "And deeper still?"
3. List out all the risks, costs, and consequences of following your desires and *this* story. Be honest about everything and everyone that can so easily (and legitimately) get in your way.
4. Which of those listed obstacles perpetuate and reinforce the stories you've been told and the ones you've told yourself? How do they differ from the story you *know* is true, the one you desire and deserve?
5. What is the smallest possible step that you can take toward the story you long for? Take it. And then one more. And another one after that. Bit by bit is more than acceptable. Nothing earth-shattering, at least to start. No apple carts to turn over, at least yet. Maybe just a single and oh-so-delicious bite of fruit.
6. Give yourself permission to write out the story you long to live, the legacy you'd love to leave, the things that matter most. Compare this to the stories you've been told and the ones you tell yourself. Celebrate just how different they are from one another. Acknowledge the rewriting you've already done.

7. Remember, yet again, that you are never alone—that you are infinitely surrounded and supported by women *who proudly claim you* as their own: their daughter, their lineage, their kin.

ACKNOWLEDGMENTS

How does one begin to express all the conversations, decisions, paths, journeys, and people that have woven themselves into my life, my story, and this book? I cannot, of course. But this is my heartfelt attempt.

When I decided to move years of writing into published form, She Writes Press—a publishing company exclusively for women, trans, and nonbinary authors—was the logical and perfect choice. Such care has been taken with the biggest and smallest of things: the title, the cover art, the typesetting, the behind-the-scenes decisions about shelf placement, genre, SEO, and so much more. I am deeply grateful that you have midwifed what I've been laboring to birth for so very long. Special thanks to Brooke Warner, Krissa Lagos, and Lauren Wise—the three of you beautifully held and supported this book's long-awaited delivery with tenderness and grace.

Decades ago, when I started my Master of Divinity degree, one man called forth my voice as a woman, a thought leader, and a storyteller. Paul Steinke, I am in your debt. Your faith in me, your heart on my behalf, and what you believed in even when I did not has made this book possible.

I am indebted to so many peers, colleagues, and clients who have generously and tenderly shared their stories with me and demonstrated, in the most beautiful of ways, the inspiring and enduring power of women. You have affirmed, challenged, and supported me. You have shaped and changed the woman I have become.

There are three women who have stood alongside and stayed through my every declaration and doubt, argument and apology, stumble and fall, strength and celebration. Tanya Geisler, Andrea Olson, and Nancy Swanson—I cannot see a way in which this day would have ever come to be if not for your steadfastness, faith, friendship, and love.

Dad, I wish you were still alive to celebrate this day with me. I can picture your face, see your tears, and feel the way your heart would jump out of your chest in pride. Mom, it has been your faithful conviction to these stories, the text within which they abide, and the God you so deeply love that has engraved them on my heart.

Tom and Grace: It has meant everything to have you just down a flight of stairs as I've written, edited, and written some more. Your excitement has buoyed me, and your selfless care has given me more rest and encouragement than you could ever know. Thank you.

Lorri, my sister and best/truest friend: You have taught me what it means to love in fierce, enduring, and unconditional ways. When I think about the power of women's stories, it is ours that always comes to mind and heart first. Who would I be without you?

My daughters, Emma Joy and Abby Evangeline: For all the words I write and speak, they fall woefully short when it comes to you. You have been, are, and forever will be my whole heart, my whole world, my everything. I love you.

And finally, to the eleven women of whom I have written in these pages: I am infinitely grateful and so deeply honored to tell your stories, imagine your voices, and reveal your hearts. I have felt your hands on my back, holding me steady and pushing me forward. I have heard you whisper (and sometimes shout) in my ears, calling me to you again and again. I have leaned on your presence, your strength, your wisdom, and your endless, endless hope that somehow, someday, I might make you known in the powerful and poignant ways you have always desired and most certainly have deserved. I hope you are pleased.

IF YOU LOVED
REWRITING EVE

A book like this becomes "known" via word of mouth. Here are five specific actions that are incredibly helpful:

1. Review *Rewriting Eve* on Amazon and Goodreads. Though any and every review is more than welcome, these two sites are the most important related to sales.

2. Tell anyone and everyone about *Rewriting Eve*. Post a recommendation on social media, in your newsletter or blog, and within any groups you are part of. And of course, talk about it with family, friends, and colleagues!

3. Ask your local library and/or bookstore to carry the book.

4. Recommend me as a guest for podcasts, TV and radio shows, newsletters, blogs, or other social-media related forums. Copy-ready images and content: https://ronnadetrick.com/rewriting-eve-media

5. I'd love to join you on Zoom for a discussion about *Rewriting Eve*. Gather 6+ people in your book club / church group / women's gathering / women's retreat / support group and I'll be there! Details: https:// ronnadetrick.com/bookclubs

Thanks so much for supporting me in these ways. It makes all the difference. You do!

NOTES

Introduction

1. Christina Baldwin, *Storycatcher: Making Sense of Our Lives through the Power and Practice of Story* (Novato, CA: New World Library, 2005), 9–10.

2. Neil Gaiman, *M Is for Magic* (New York: Harper Collins, reprint edition 2008), 7.

3. Sharon Blackie, *If Women Rose Rooted: A Life-changing Journey to Authenticity and Belonging* (Tewkesbury, England: September Publishing, 2019), 198.

4. Elizabeth Lesser, *Cassandra Speaks: When Women Are the Storytellers, the Human Story Changes* (New York: Harper Wave, 2022), 20.

5. Adrienne Rich, "When We Dead Awaken: Writing as Re-Vision," *College English*, Vol. 34, No. 1, Women, Writing and Teaching, October, 1972, (National Council of Teachers of English), 18–30.

6. Wilda C. Gafney, *Womanist Midrash on the Torah: A Reintroduction to the Women of the Torah and the Throne* (Louisville, KY: Westminster John Knox Press, 2017), 9.

7. Rachel Held-Evans, *A Year of Biblical Womanhood: How a Liberated Woman Found Herself Sitting on Her Roof, Covering Her Head, and Calling Her Husband 'Master'* (Nashville, TN: Thomas Nelson, 2012).

8. Sara Bessey, *Out of Sorts: Making Peace with an Evolving Faith* (Brentwood, TN: Howard Books, 2015).

Chapter One: Eve

1. Sally Roesh Wagner, "Women's History Month Myths," the *New York Times*, March 1, 2019, www.nytimes.com/2019/03/01 /us/womens-history-month-myths.html.
2. Danielle Dulsky, *The Holy Wild: A Heathen Bible for the Untamed Woman* (Novato, CA: New World Library, 2018), 3.
3. Ibid, 27.
4. Glennon Doyle, *Untamed* (New York: The Dial Press, 2020), 122.
5. Pat McKissack, *Sojourner Truth: A Voice for Freedom (Great African Americans Series)* (New Jersey: Enslow Publishing, revised edition, 2008).

Chapter Two: Cain's Wife

1. We still use the idiom "the mark of Cain" to infer disgrace or public disapproval when, ironically, it offered just the opposite.

Chapter Three: Hagar

1. Gafney, *Womanist Midrash*, 42. "The standard translations do not capture the physical violence that is represented by this verb . . . In fact, Sarai's oppression of Hagar in Genesis 16:6 is the same as Egypt's oppression of Israel in Exodus 1:11, ultimately leading to God's liberating intervention."
2. Ibid.
3. Tikva Frymer-Kensky, "Hagar" in *Women in Scripture: A Dictionary of Named and Unnamed Women in the Hebrew Bible, the Apocryphal/Deuterocanonical Books, and the New Testament*, ed. Carol Meyers, (New York: Houghton Mifflin Company, 2000), 87.
4. Gafney, *Womanist Midrash*, 43.
5. A much-quoted (and unhelpfully applied) verse when times

are hard: "All things work together for good for those who love God and fit into God's plans."

6. Clarissa Pinkola Estés, PhD, *Women Who Run with the Wolves: Myths and Stories of the Wild Woman Archetype* (New York: Ballantine Books, 1992), 5.

Chapter Four: The Midwives

1. Virginia Woolf, *A Room of One's Own* (London: Penguin Books, 1945).

2. Margaret Guenther and Alan Jones, *Holy Listening: The Art of Spiritual Direction* (Boston, MA: Cowley Publications, 1992).

3. Maya Wei-Haas, "The True Story of 'Hidden Figures,' the Forgotten Women Who Helped Win the Space Race," *Smithsonian Magazine*, September 8, 2016, www.smithsonianmag.com/history/forgotten-black-women-mathematicians-who-helped-win-wars-and-send-astronauts-space-180960393.

4. Amy Daire, "17 Incredible Women You've Never Heard of Who Changed the World," *Insider*, February 28, 2017, www.insider.com/unknown-women-who-changed-the-world-2017-2.

5. Merlin Stone, *When God Was a Woman: The Landmark Exploration of the Ancient Worship of the Great Goddess and the Eventual Suppression of Women's Rites* (New York: Houghton Mifflin Harcourt Publishing Company, 1976), 1.

6. Rebecca Solnit, *Men Explain Things to Me*, (Chicago, IL: Haymarket Books, 2015).

7. Becca De Souza, "The Motherheart of God—Becca's Story," *The She Is Project*, May 20, 2018, https://thesheisproject.org/2018/05/the-motherheart-of-god-becaas-story.

Chapter Five: Jael

1. Ijeoma Oluo, *So You Want to Talk About Race* (New York: Seal Press, 2018), 224.

2. Tikva Frymer-Kensky, *Reading the Women of the Bible: A New Interpretation of Their Stories* (New York: Schocken Books, 2002), 51–52.

3. Doyle, *Untamed*, 67.

Chapter Six: Vashti

1. Nikki Giovanni, *My House* (New York: HarperCollins, 1972).

2. "*Queen for a Day*," Wikipedia, last modified September 14, 2022, https://en.wikipedia.org/wiki/Queen_for_a_Day.

3. Stephanie Buck, "This 1950s Game Show Profited from the Poverty of a New Woman Every Day," *Timeline*, March 24, 2017, https://timeline.com/queen-for-a-day-tv-sexism-9bd594f509d9.

4. Kelly Diels, "The Female Lifestyle Empowerment Brand. An Introduction," January 4, 2016, www.kellydiels.com/female-lifestyle-empowerment-brand-introduction.

5. Ani DiFranco, *No Walls and the Recurring Dream: A Memoir* (New York: Viking Press, 2019).

6. Laurie Penney, *Unspeakable Things: Sex, Lies, and Revolution* (New York: Bloomsbury USA, 2016).

7. Nadia Bolz-Weber, *Shameless: A Sexual Reformation* (Colorado Springs, CO: Convergent Books, 2019).

Chapter Seven: Esther

1. Estés, *Women Who Run with the Wolves*, 17–18.

2. Matt Page, "Films About Esther," *Bible Films Blog*, February 16, 2006, https://biblefilms.blogspot.com/2006/02/films-about-esther.html.

3. The other book named for a woman is Ruth; The Song of Solomon is the only other book in this text that does not mention God. Interestingly, like the Book of Esther, both are nearly exclusively about a woman.

4. Sidnie White Crawford, "Esther" in *Women in Scripture*, 76.

5. Princess O'Nika Auguste, "Was Esther a Post-Colonial Feminist," *Christian Feminism Today*, March 2017, https://eewc.com/esther-post-colonial-feminist.

Chapter Eight: The Canaanite Woman

1. Soraya Chemaly, *Rage Becomes Her: The Power of Women's Anger* (New York: Simon & Schuster, 2018), xviii-xix.
2. Sara M. Moniuszko and Cara Kelly, "Harvey Weinstein Scandal: A Complete List of the 87 Accusers," *USA Today*, October 27, 2017, https://www.usatoday.com/story/life/people/2017/10/27/weinstein-scandal-complete-list-accusers/804663001.
3. Donald Brown, "Is the Super Bowl the Largest Human Trafficking Event in the World?" *International Justice Mission*, https://www.ijm.org/news/is-the-super-bowl-the-largest-human-trafficking-event-in-the-world.
4. Caroline Criado Perez, *Invisible Women: Data Bias in a World Designed for Men* (New York: Abrams Books, 2019).
5. Estés, *Women Who Run with the Wolves.*
6. Wendy Farley, *The Wounding and Healing of Desire: Weaving Heaven and Earth* (Louisville, KY: Westminster John Knox Press, 2005).
7. Amy Jill-Levine, "The Canaanite Woman" in *Women in Scripture*, 413.
8. Lynn H. Cohick, "The Canaanite Woman of Matthew 15," *Zondervan Academic Blog*, October 21, 2008, https://zondervanacademic.com/blog/the-caanite-w.
9. Thomas Merton, *No Man Is an Island* (Boulder, CO: Shambhala, 2005), 245.
10. Rachel Held-Evans and Jeff Chu, *Wholehearted Faith* (San Francisco: Harper One, 2022), 98–99.
11. Ibid, 145.

Chapter Nine: The Woman at the Well

1. Erica Jong, *Fear of Flying: 40ᵗʰ Anniversary Edition* (New York: Open Road Integrated Media, 2013), 187.
2. Dr. Brené Brown, *Atlas of the Heart: Mapping Meaningful Connection and the Language of Human Experience* (New York: Random House, 2021), 137.
3. Craig S. Farmer, "Changing Images of the Samaritan Woman in Early Reformed Commentaries on John," *Church History*, Vol. 65. No. 3 (Cambridge, England: Cambridge University Press, 1996), 365–375.
4. The Gospel of Mary, a non-canonical text that was discovered in 1896, provides us the story and theology of Mary Magdalene. It unequivocally names and honors her as Jesus's equal, his thought partner, the one in whom he confides his deepest truths. Within the canon, the Woman at the Well holds this distinction.

Chapter Ten: The Woman of Revelation 12

1. Tina Pippin, "Woman in Labor, Clothed with the Sun" in *Women in Scripture*, 544.
2. C. S. Lewis, *The Last Battle: Chronicles of Narnia Book 7* (New York: Harper Collins, Reprint Edition, 2002), 195–197.

Afterword: Rewriting You

1. Carolyn See, *Making a Literary Life: Advice for Writers and Other Dreamers* (New York: Ballantine Books, 2003).
2. Chimamanda Ngozi Adichie, "The Danger of a Single Story," Ted Global, 2009, https://www.ted.com/talks/chimamanda_ngozi_adichie_the_danger_of_a_single_story.
3. Blackie, *If Women Rose Rooted*, 39.

ABOUT THE AUTHOR

RONNA DETRICK left the church and its dogma nearly twenty years ago but took the stories of women with her. She has combined her love of writing with a diverse and winding career that has included coaching, spiritual direction, professional development training, corporate leadership, and entrepreneurship. She shocked and delighted her audience in a provocative TEDx presentation on an Eve who inspires and empowers women instead of shaming and silencing them. She holds both a Master of Divinity degree and a Certificate in Spiritual Direction from The Seattle School of Theology and Psychology and a B.A. in Business and Communications from Whitworth University. After living most of her life in the Pacific Northwest, she is now just minutes from the Atlantic Ocean in Hampstead, NC, where she continues to write, drink strong coffee, have beautiful conversations with her clients, and cannot be dissuaded from the belief that her two daughters are the most amazing humans on the planet. Learn more at ronnadetrick.com.

Author photo by Emma Joy Miller

SELECTED TITLES FROM SHE WRITES PRESS

She Writes Press is an independent publishing company founded to serve women writers everywhere. Visit us at www.shewritespress.com.

Amazon Wisdom Keeper: A Psychologist's Memoir of Spiritual Awakening, Loraine Y. Van Tuyl, PhD. $16.95, 978-1-63152-316-8. Van Tuyl, a graduate psychology student and budding shamanic healer, is blindsided when she begins to experience startling visions, hear elusive drumming, and become aware of her inseverable, mystical ties to the Amazon rainforest of her native Suriname. Is she in the wrong field, or did her childhood dreams, imaginary guides, and premonitions somehow prepare her for these challenges?

Beyond Jesus: My Spiritual Odyssey by Patricia A. Pearce. $16.95, 978-1-63152-359-5. In the crucible of grief following a friend's death, Patricia Pearce resolved to open herself to hidden dimensions of her existence—not realizing her quest would cost her her vocation as a Presbyterian pastor, open her eyes to the radical implications of Jesus's message, and uncover what she believes is the key to our spiritual evolution.

Finding Venerable Mother: A Daughter's Spiritual Quest to Thailand by Cindy Rasicot. $16.95, 978-1-63152-702-9. In midlife, Cindy travels halfway around the world to Thailand and unexpectedly discovers a Thai Buddhist nun who offers her the unconditional love and acceptance her own mother was never able to provide. This soulful and engaging memoir reminds readers that when we go forward with a truly open heart, faith, forgiveness, and love are all possible.

Just Be: A Search for Self-Love in India by Meredith Rom. $16.95, 978-1-63152-286-4. After following her intuition to fly across the world and travel alone through the crowded streets of India, twenty-two-year-old Meredith Rom learns that that true spiritual development begins when we take the leap of trusting our intuition and finding a love within.

Living a Spiritual Life in a Material World: 4 Keys to Fulfillment and Balance by Anna Gatmon, PhD. $16.95, 978-1-63152-256-7. Dr. Anna Gatmon demystifies the all-too-often elusive nature of spirituality and brings it down to earth, providing a concrete roadmap to living a life that is spiritually fulfilling without having to give up material pleasures.

Serious Little Catholics: A Memoir by Kathy Gereau. $16.95, 978-1-64742-110-6. A hilarious peek into the Catholic school experience through the eyes of Kathy Gereau—who, by learning to laugh at the ridiculous bits of dogma, eventually finds the spiritual message within.